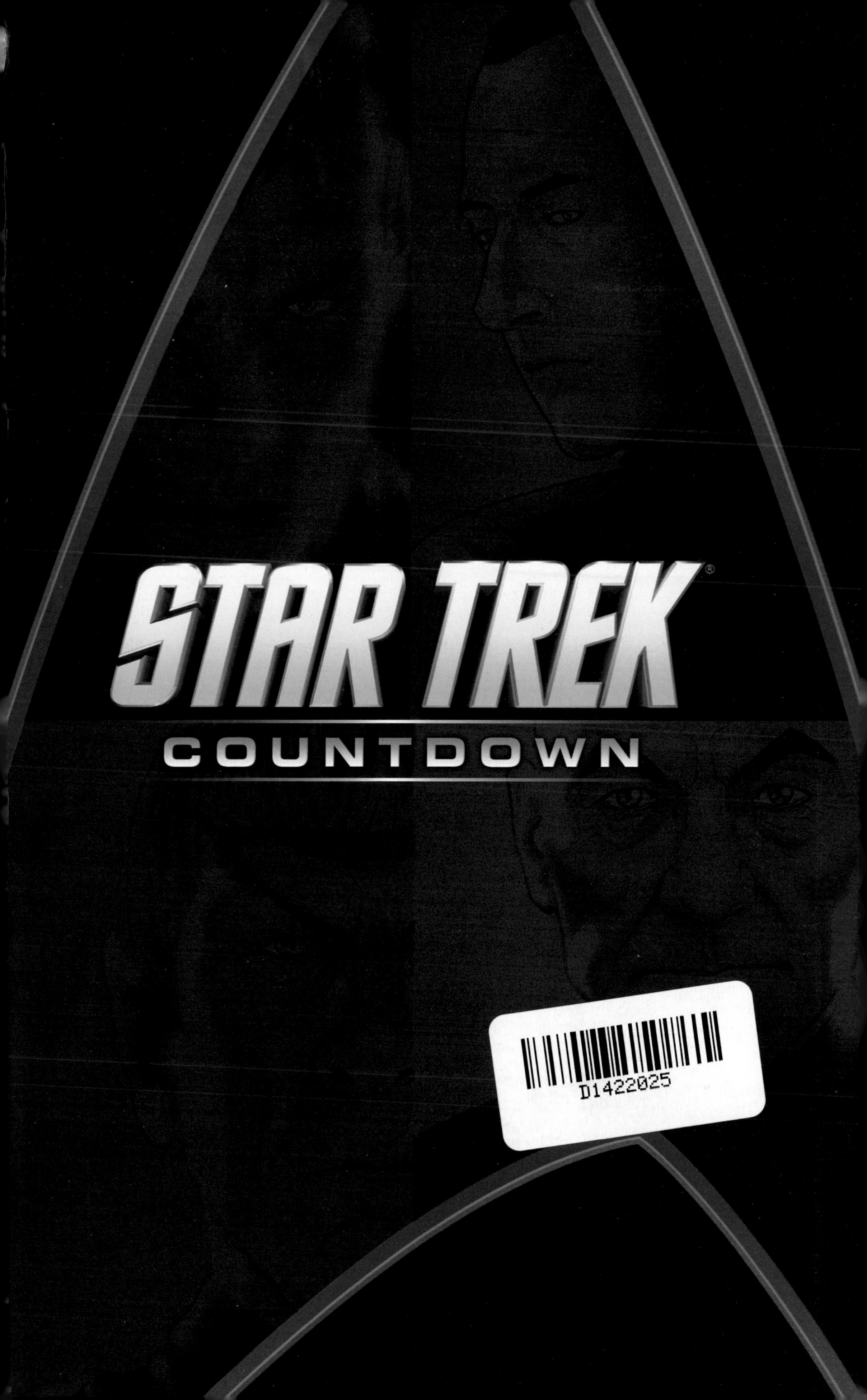
STAR TREK®
COUNTDOWN

STAR TREK®
COUNTDOWN

Story
Roberto Orci & Alex Kurtzman

Writers
Mike Johnson & Tim Jones

Artist
David Messina

Color Art
Giovanna Niro

Additional Colors
David Messina and Paolo Maddaleni

Color Consultant
Ilaria Traversi

Letterers
Chris Mowry, Robert Robbins, and Neil Uyetake

Creative Consultant
David Baronoff

Original Series Editors
Andy Schmidt and Scott Dunbier

Collection Editor
Justin Eisinger

Collection Designer
Neil Uyetake

www.TITANBOOKS.com www.IDWPUBLISHING.com
ISBN: 9781848564350

STAR TREK created by Gene Roddenberry

Special Thanks to Risa Kessler and John Van Citters at CBS Consumer Products, JJ Abrams and Bryan Burk at Bad Robot Productions, Mandy Safavi, Ben Kim, Pete Chiarelli, Kim Cavyan, Steven Puri and Rafael Ruthchild at K/O Productions, and Elena Casagrande, Rick Sternbach and Scott Tipton for their invaluable assistance. Additionally, David Messina would like to thank his girlfriend Sara for all her love and support.

Printed in Spain. First printing: April 2008
10 9 8 7 6 5 4 3 2

Originally published as STAR TREK: COUNTDOWN Issues #1–4.

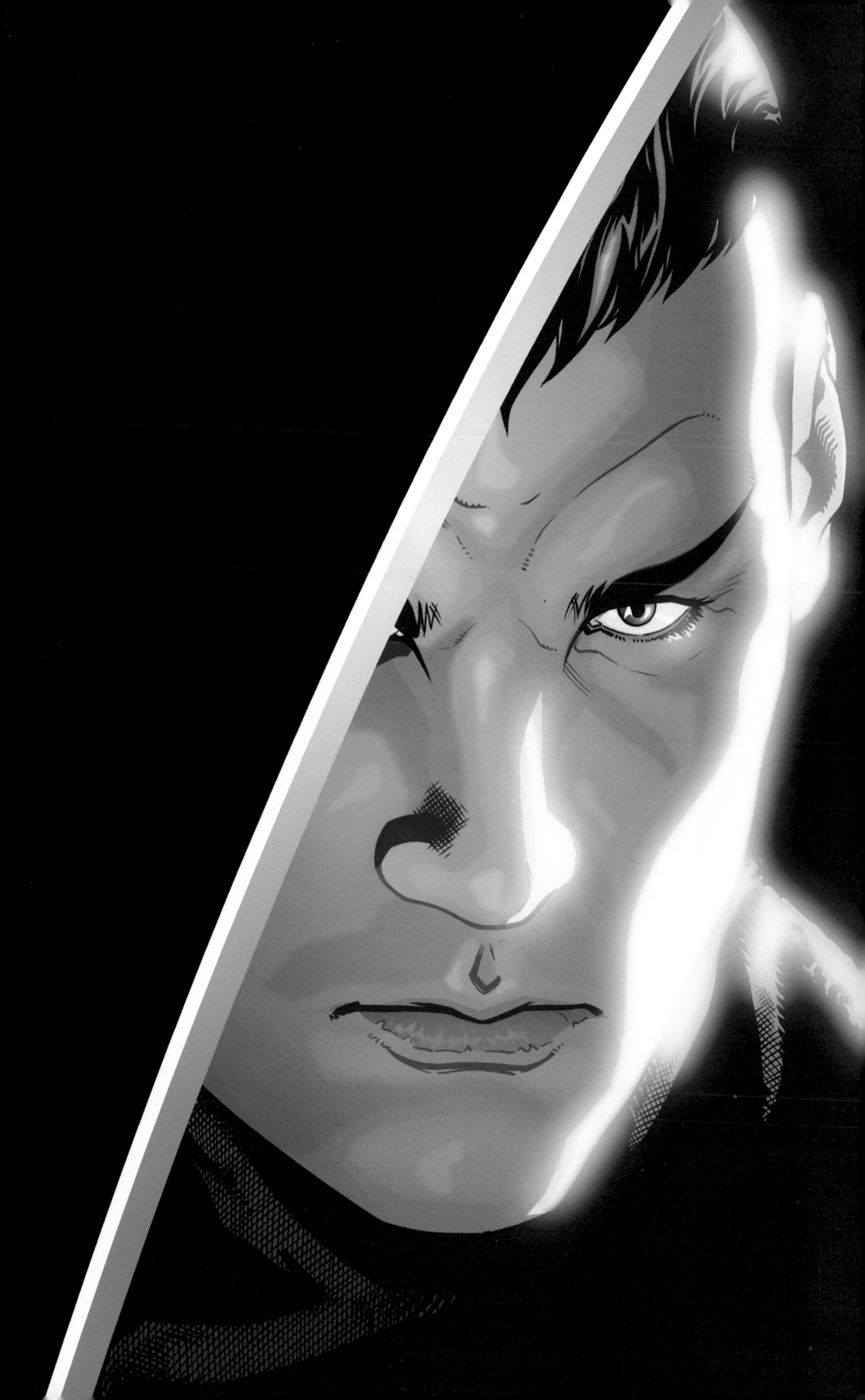

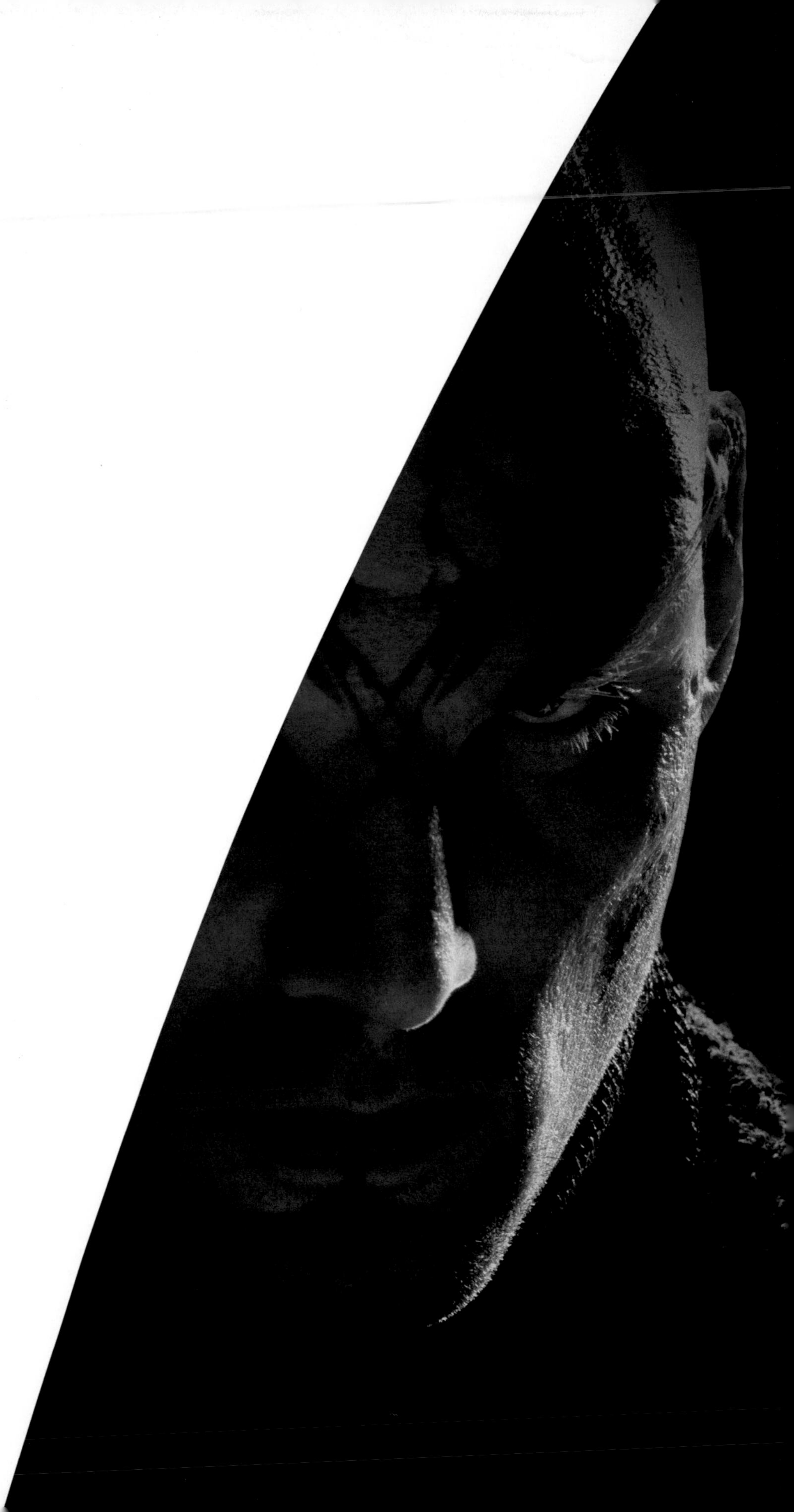

STARDATE 64333.4

DEEP IN ROMULAN
TERRITORY...

WHERE ONLY A FEW HAVE
GONE BEFORE...

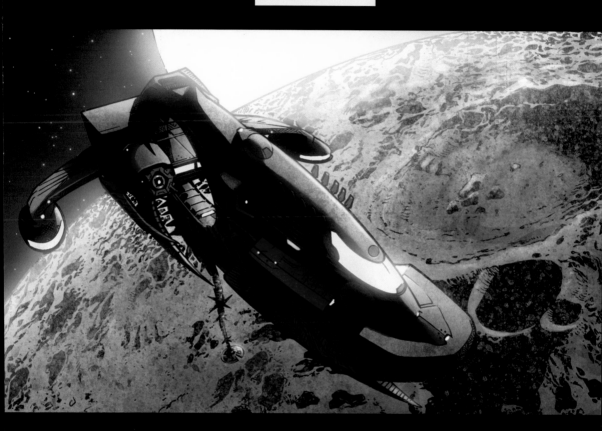

STAR TREK

COUNTDOWN

NUMBER ONE

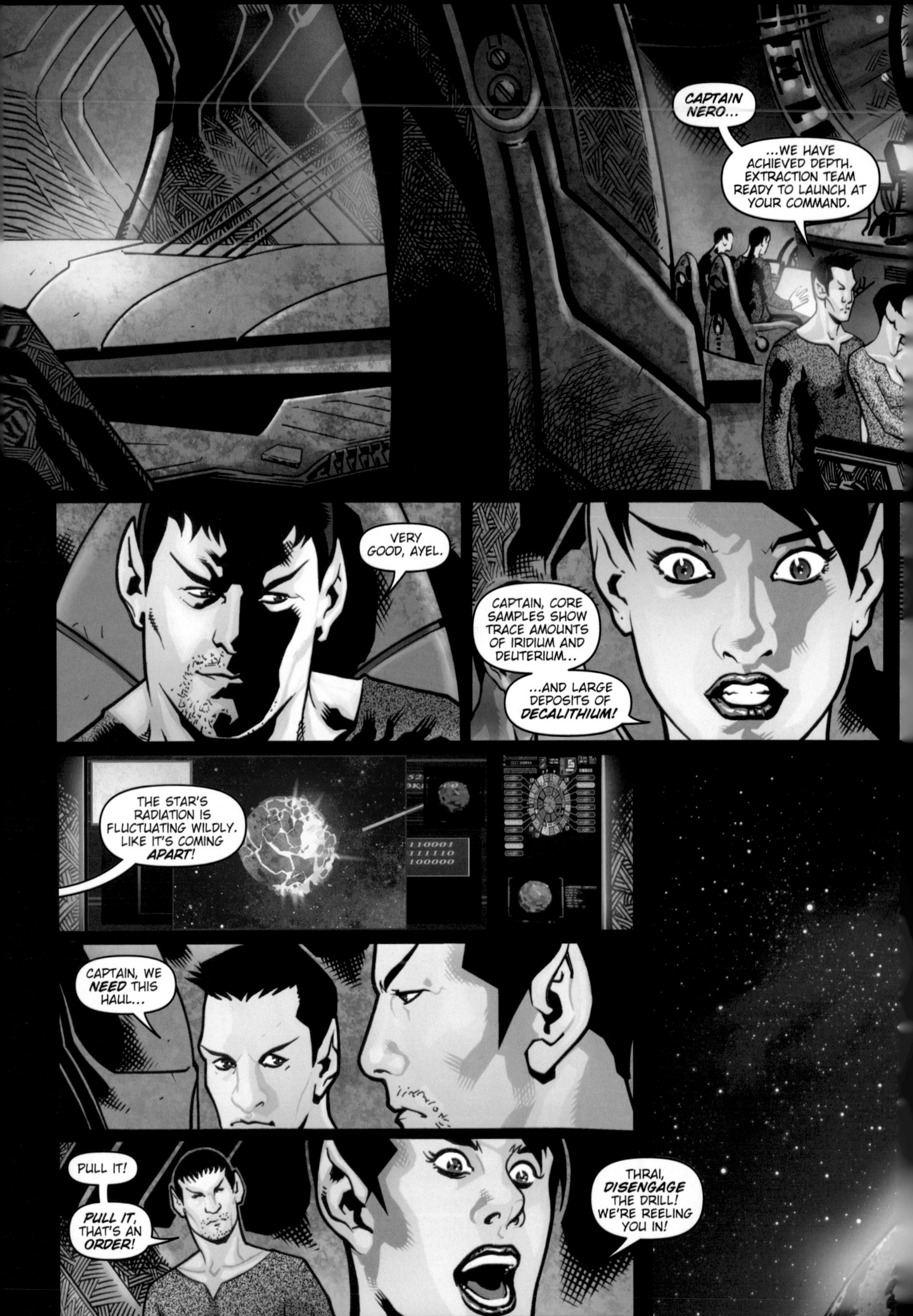
CAPTAIN NERO...
...WE HAVE ACHIEVED DEPTH. EXTRACTION TEAM READY TO LAUNCH AT YOUR COMMAND.
VERY GOOD, AYEL.
CAPTAIN, CORE SAMPLES SHOW TRACE AMOUNTS OF IRIDIUM AND DEUTERIUM...
...AND LARGE DEPOSITS OF DECALITHIUM!
THE STAR'S RADIATION IS FLUCTUATING WILDLY. LIKE IT'S COMING APART!
110001
111110
100000
CAPTAIN, WE NEED THIS HAUL...
PULL IT!
PULL IT, THAT'S AN ORDER!
THRAI, DISENGAGE THE DRILL! WE'RE REELING YOU IN!

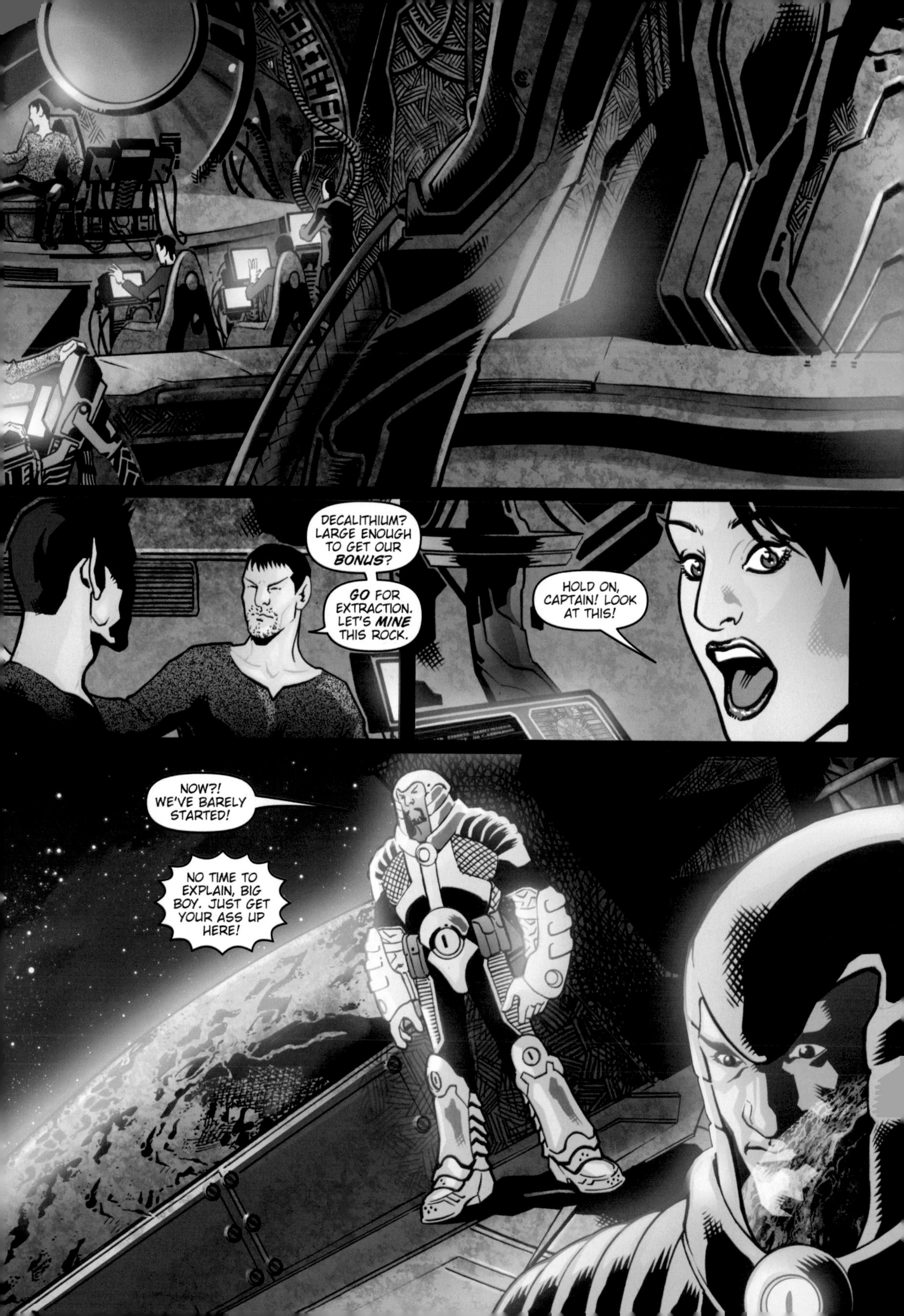
DECALITHIUM? LARGE ENOUGH TO GET OUR BONUS?
GO FOR EXTRACTION. LET'S MINE THIS ROCK.
HOLD ON, CAPTAIN! LOOK AT THIS!
NOW?! WE'VE BARELY STARTED!
NO TIME TO EXPLAIN, BIG BOY. JUST GET YOUR ASS UP HERE!

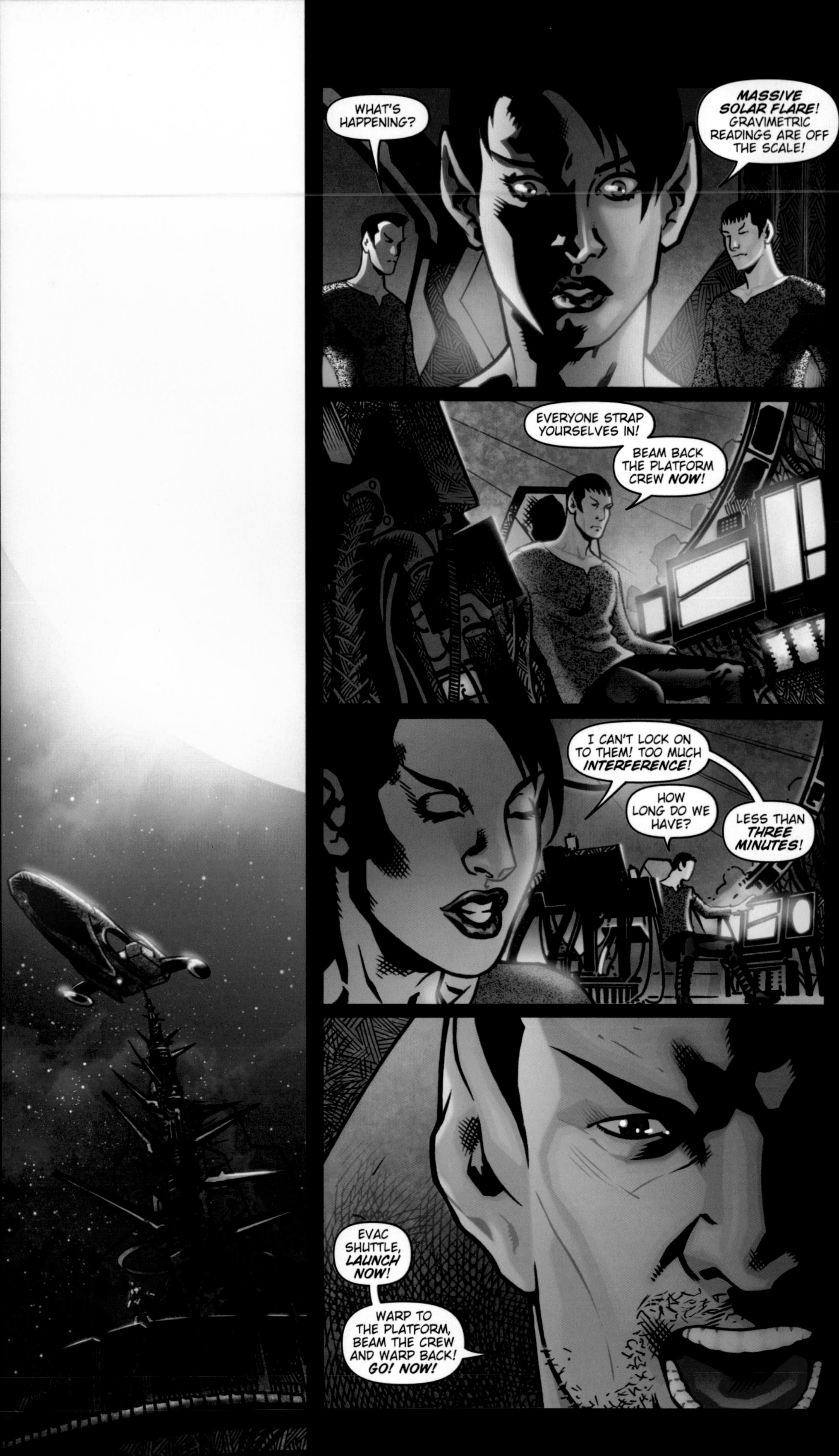

WHAT'S HAPPENING?
MASSIVE SOLAR FLARE! GRAVIMETRIC READINGS ARE OFF THE SCALE!
EVERYONE STRAP YOURSELVES IN!
BEAM BACK THE PLATFORM CREW NOW!
I CAN'T LOCK ON TO THEM! TOO MUCH INTERFERENCE!
HOW LONG DO WE HAVE?
LESS THAN THREE MINUTES!
EVAC SHUTTLE, LAUNCH NOW!
WARP TO THE PLATFORM, BEAM THE CREW AND WARP BACK! GO! NOW!

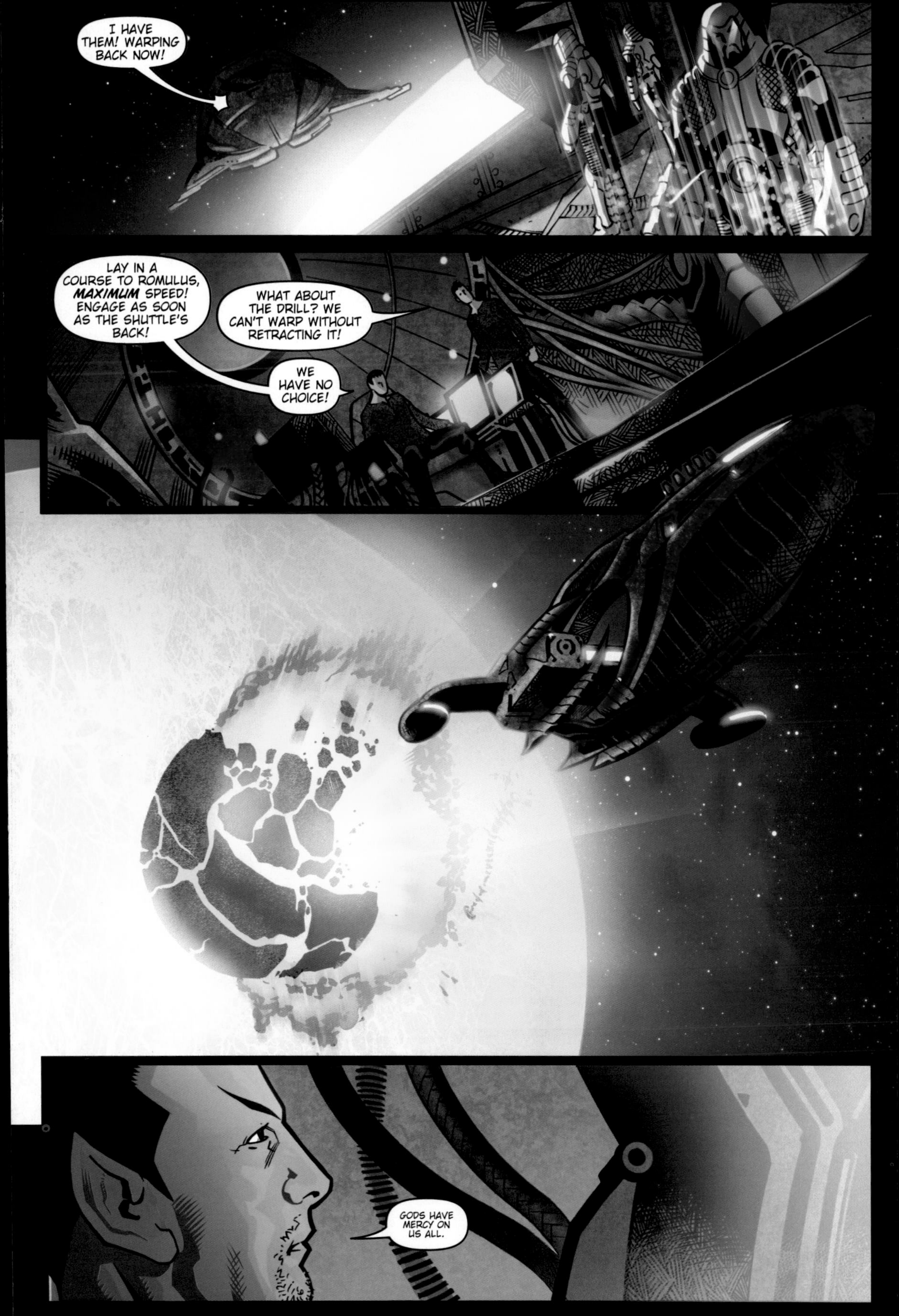
I HAVE THEM! WARPING BACK NOW!
LAY IN A COURSE TO ROMULUS, MAXIMUM SPEED! ENGAGE AS SOON AS THE SHUTTLE'S BACK!
WHAT ABOUT THE DRILL? WE CAN'T WARP WITHOUT RETRACTING IT!
WE HAVE NO CHOICE!
GODS HAVE MERCY ON US ALL.

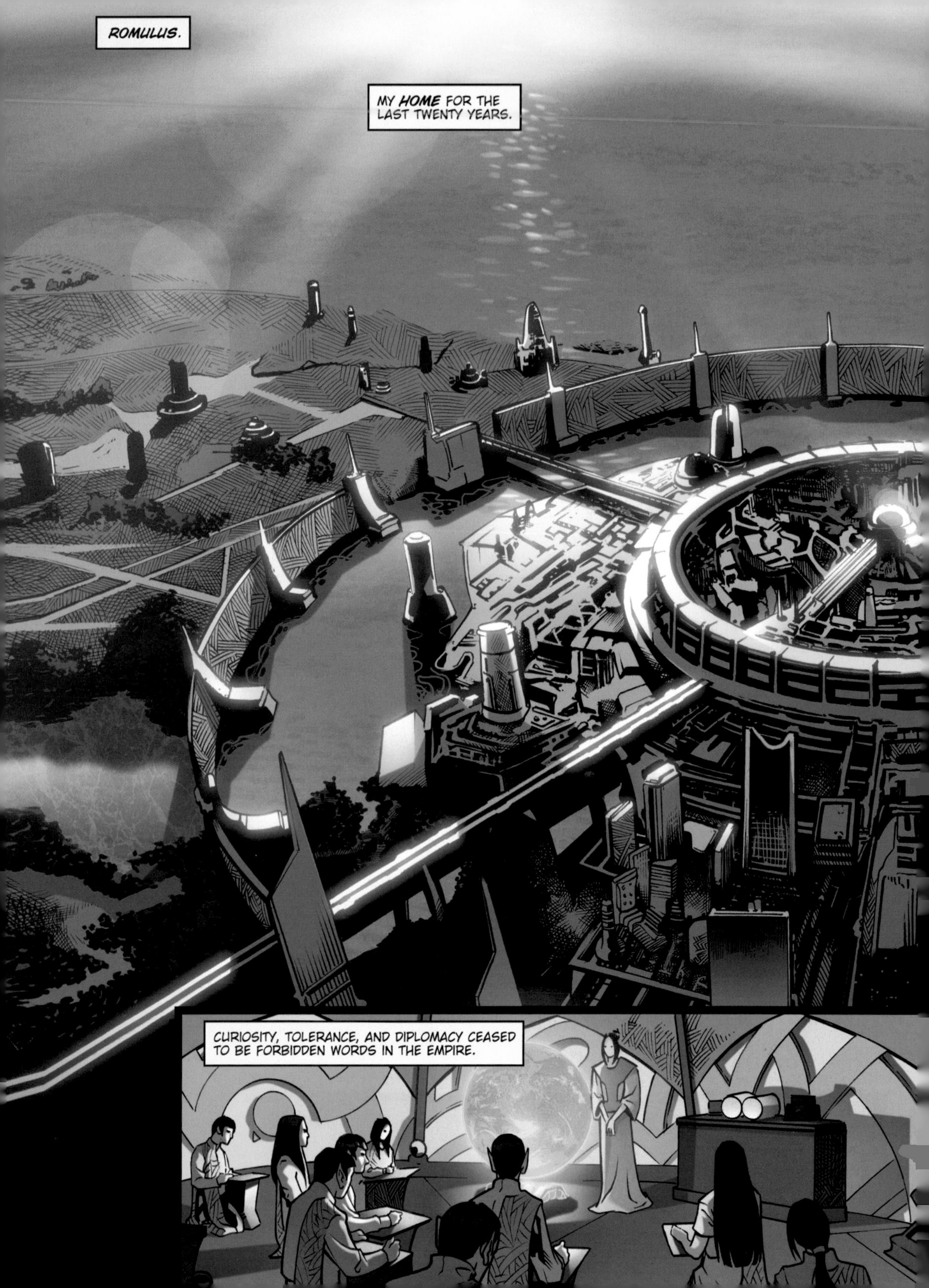
ROMULUS.
MY HOME FOR THE LAST TWENTY YEARS.
CURIOSITY, TOLERANCE, AND DIPLOMACY CEASED TO BE FORBIDDEN WORDS IN THE EMPIRE.

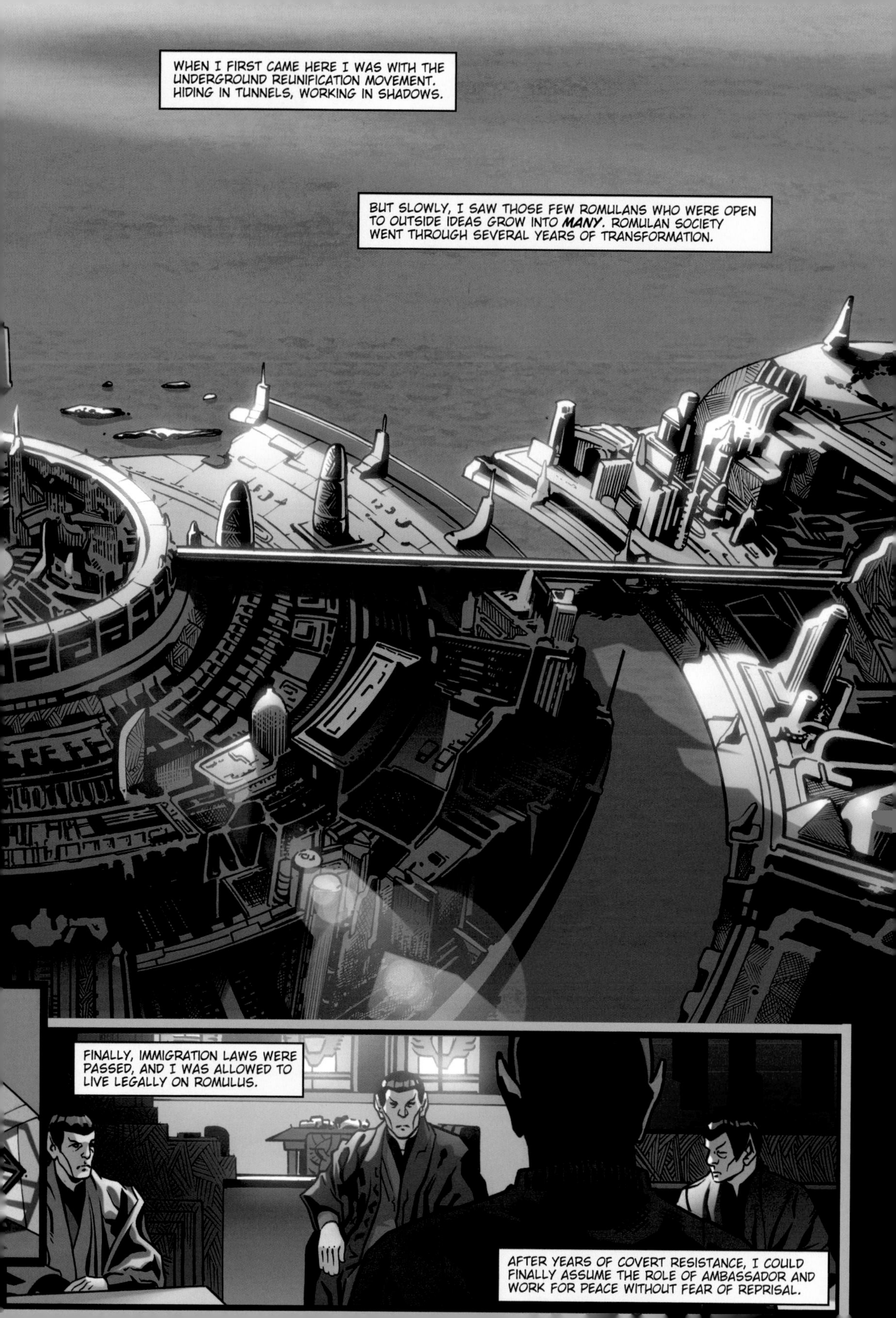
WHEN I FIRST CAME HERE I WAS WITH THE UNDERGROUND REUNIFICATION MOVEMENT. HIDING IN TUNNELS, WORKING IN SHADOWS.
BUT SLOWLY, I SAW THOSE FEW ROMULANS WHO WERE OPEN TO OUTSIDE IDEAS GROW INTO MANY. ROMULAN SOCIETY WENT THROUGH SEVERAL YEARS OF TRANSFORMATION.
FINALLY, IMMIGRATION LAWS WERE PASSED, AND I WAS ALLOWED TO LIVE LEGALLY ON ROMULUS.
AFTER YEARS OF COVERT RESISTANCE, I COULD FINALLY ASSUME THE ROLE OF AMBASSADOR AND WORK FOR PEACE WITHOUT FEAR OF REPRISAL.

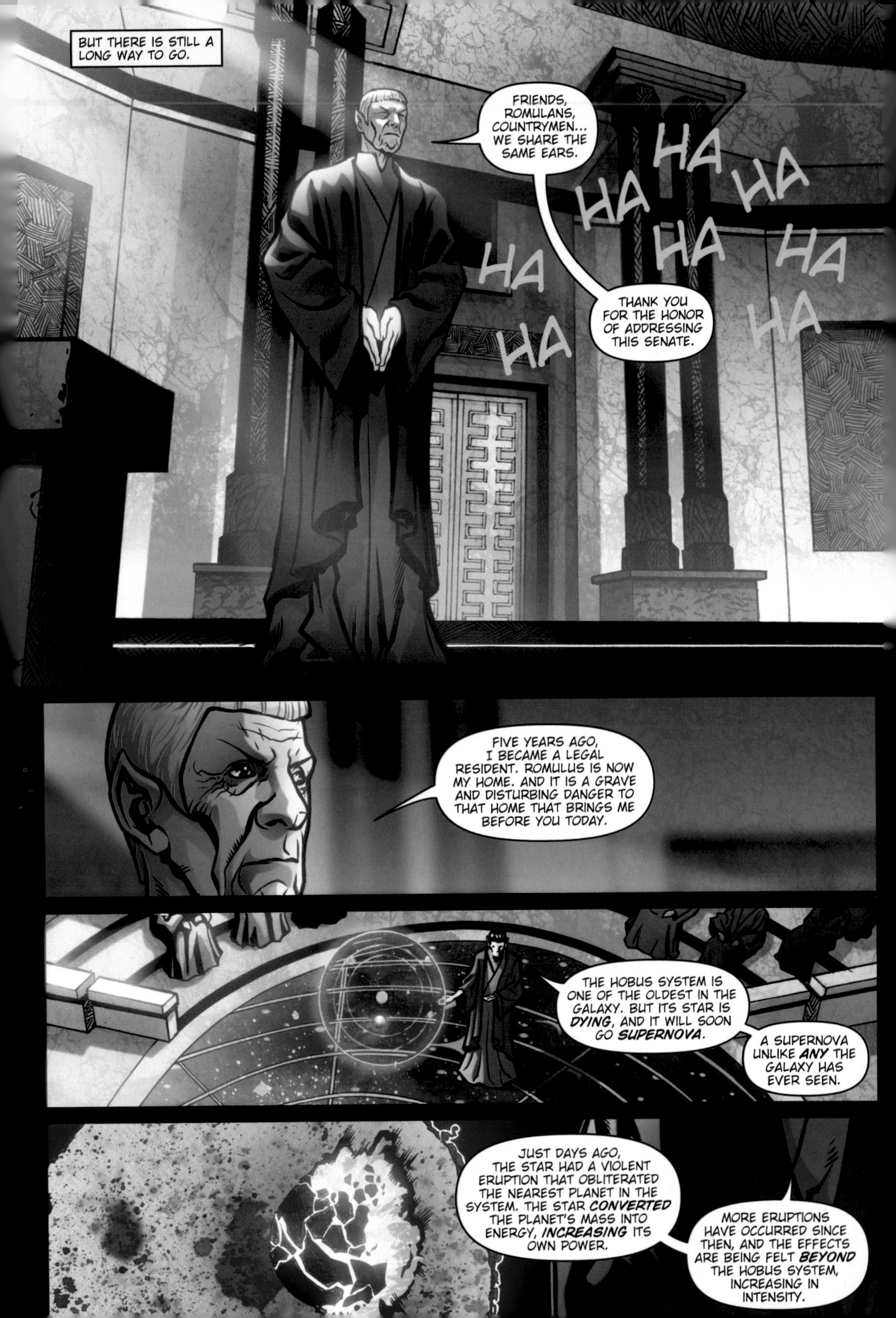
BUT THERE IS STILL A LONG WAY TO GO.
FRIENDS, ROMULANS, COUNTRYMEN... WE SHARE THE SAME EARS.
HA HA HA HA HA HA HA HA HA
THANK YOU FOR THE HONOR OF ADDRESSING THIS SENATE.
FIVE YEARS AGO, I BECAME A LEGAL RESIDENT. ROMULUS IS NOW MY HOME. AND IT IS A GRAVE AND DISTURBING DANGER TO THAT HOME THAT BRINGS ME BEFORE YOU TODAY.
THE HOBUS SYSTEM IS ONE OF THE OLDEST IN THE GALAXY. BUT ITS STAR IS ***DYING***, AND IT WILL SOON GO ***SUPERNOVA***.
A SUPERNOVA UNLIKE ***ANY*** THE GALAXY HAS EVER SEEN.
JUST DAYS AGO, THE STAR HAD A VIOLENT ERUPTION THAT OBLITERATED THE NEAREST PLANET IN THE SYSTEM. THE STAR ***CONVERTED*** THE PLANET'S MASS INTO ENERGY, ***INCREASING*** ITS OWN POWER.
MORE ERUPTIONS HAVE OCCURRED SINCE THEN, AND THE EFFECTS ARE BEING FELT ***BEYOND*** THE HOBUS SYSTEM, INCREASING IN INTENSITY.

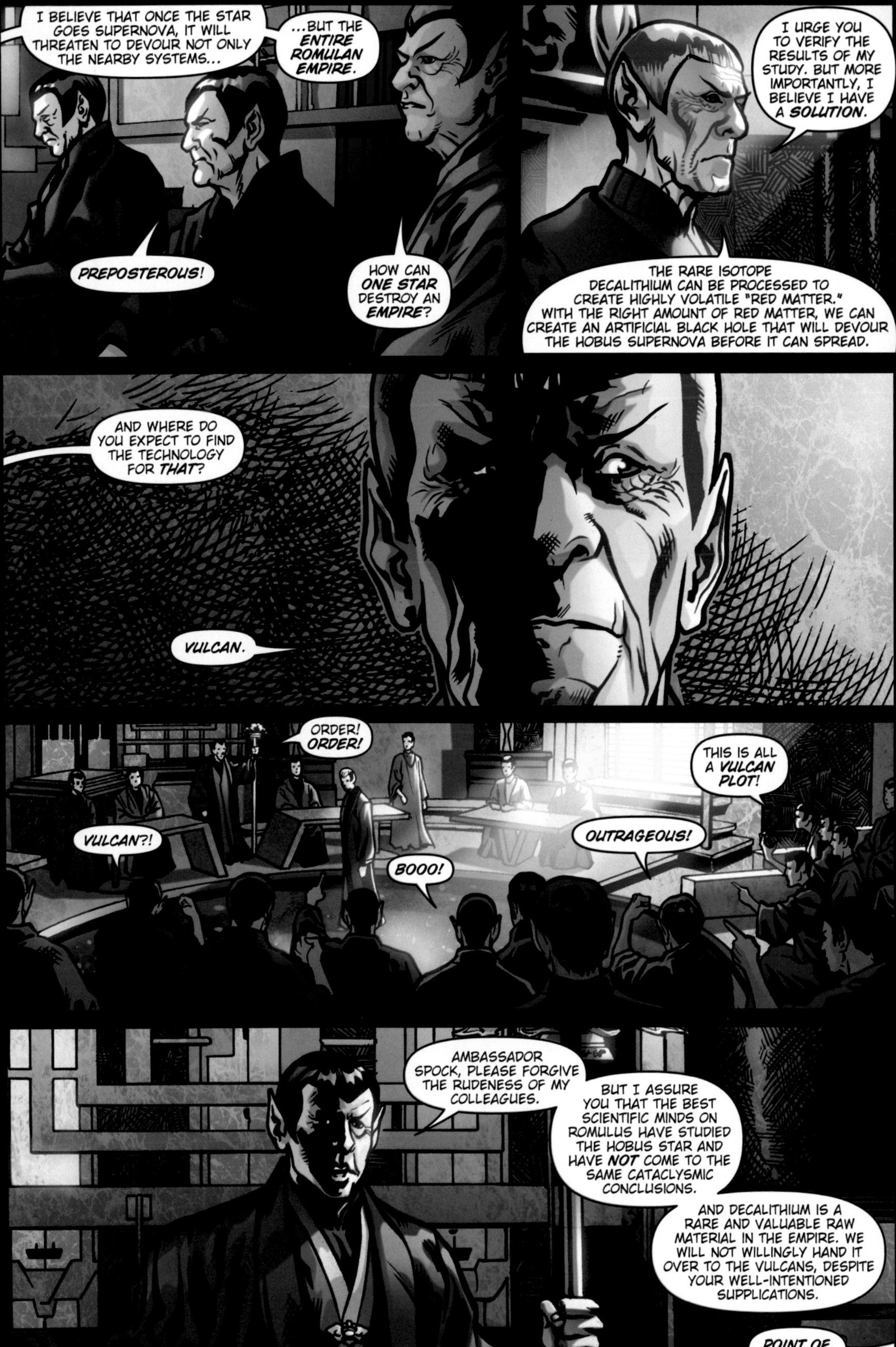
I BELIEVE THAT ONCE THE STAR GOES SUPERNOVA, IT WILL THREATEN TO DEVOUR NOT ONLY THE NEARBY SYSTEMS...
...BUT THE ENTIRE ROMULAN EMPIRE.
PREPOSTEROUS!
HOW CAN ONE STAR DESTROY AN EMPIRE?
I URGE YOU TO VERIFY THE RESULTS OF MY STUDY. BUT MORE IMPORTANTLY, I BELIEVE I HAVE A SOLUTION.
THE RARE ISOTOPE DECALITHIUM CAN BE PROCESSED TO CREATE HIGHLY VOLATILE "RED MATTER." WITH THE RIGHT AMOUNT OF RED MATTER, WE CAN CREATE AN ARTIFICIAL BLACK HOLE THAT WILL DEVOUR THE HOBUS SUPERNOVA BEFORE IT CAN SPREAD.
AND WHERE DO YOU EXPECT TO FIND THE TECHNOLOGY FOR THAT?
VULCAN.
ORDER! ORDER!
THIS IS ALL A VULCAN PLOT!
VULCAN?!
OUTRAGEOUS!
BOOO!
AMBASSADOR SPOCK, PLEASE FORGIVE THE RUDENESS OF MY COLLEAGUES.
BUT I ASSURE YOU THAT THE BEST SCIENTIFIC MINDS ON ROMULUS HAVE STUDIED THE HOBUS STAR AND HAVE NOT COME TO THE SAME CATACLYSMIC CONCLUSIONS.
AND DECALITHIUM IS A RARE AND VALUABLE RAW MATERIAL IN THE EMPIRE. WE WILL NOT WILLINGLY HAND IT OVER TO THE VULCANS, DESPITE YOUR WELL-INTENTIONED SUPPLICATIONS.
POINT OF ORDER!

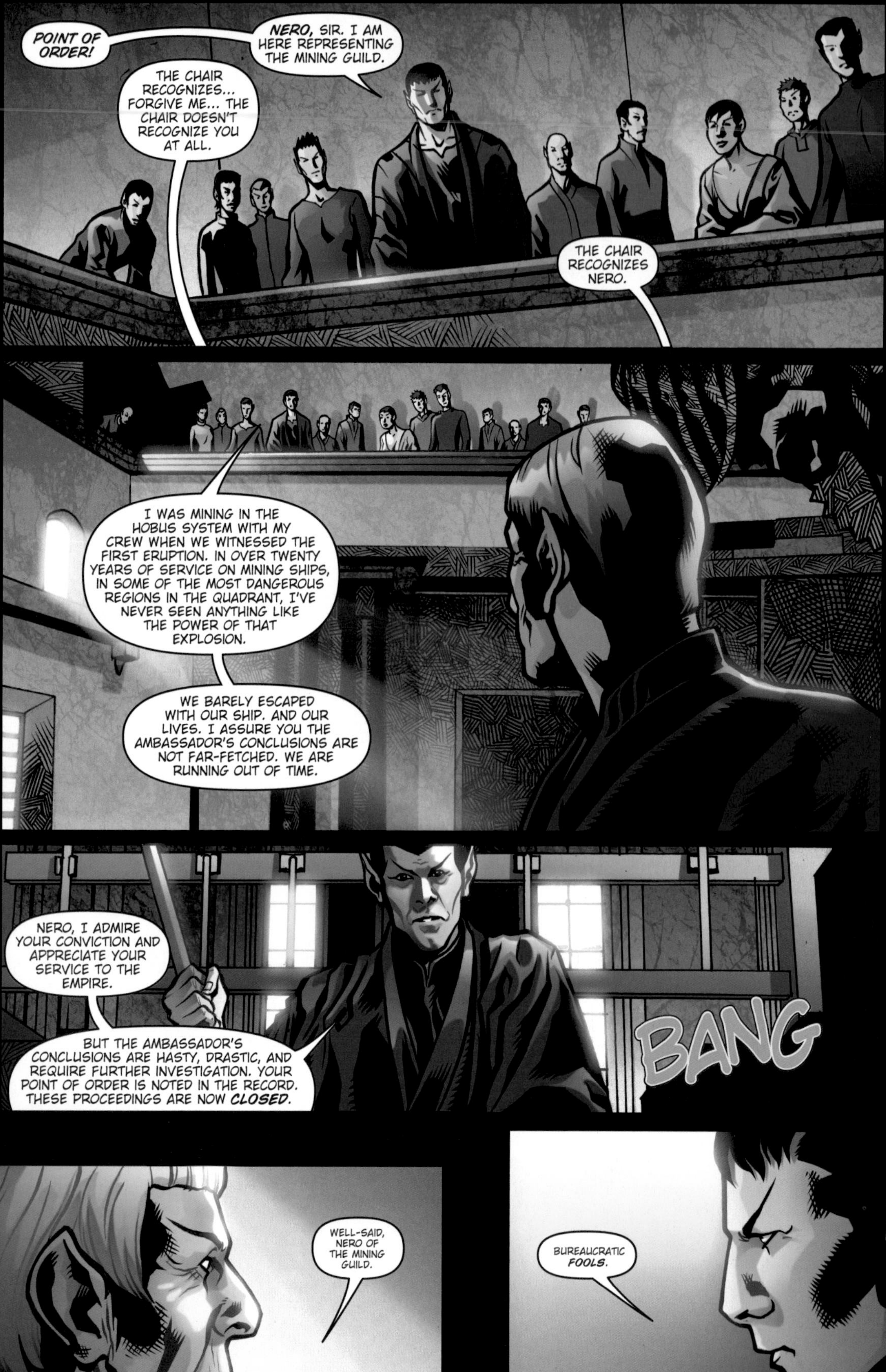

POINT OF ORDER!
NERO, SIR. I AM HERE REPRESENTING THE MINING GUILD.
THE CHAIR RECOGNIZES... FORGIVE ME... THE CHAIR DOESN'T RECOGNIZE YOU AT ALL.
THE CHAIR RECOGNIZES NERO.
I WAS MINING IN THE HOBUS SYSTEM WITH MY CREW WHEN WE WITNESSED THE FIRST ERUPTION. IN OVER TWENTY YEARS OF SERVICE ON MINING SHIPS, IN SOME OF THE MOST DANGEROUS REGIONS IN THE QUADRANT, I'VE NEVER SEEN ANYTHING LIKE THE POWER OF THAT EXPLOSION.
WE BARELY ESCAPED WITH OUR SHIP. AND OUR LIVES. I ASSURE YOU THE AMBASSADOR'S CONCLUSIONS ARE NOT FAR-FETCHED. WE ARE RUNNING OUT OF TIME.
NERO, I ADMIRE YOUR CONVICTION AND APPRECIATE YOUR SERVICE TO THE EMPIRE.
BUT THE AMBASSADOR'S CONCLUSIONS ARE HASTY, DRASTIC, AND REQUIRE FURTHER INVESTIGATION. YOUR POINT OF ORDER IS NOTED IN THE RECORD. THESE PROCEEDINGS ARE NOW CLOSED.
BANG
WELL-SAID, NERO OF THE MINING GUILD.
BUREAUCRATIC FOOLS.

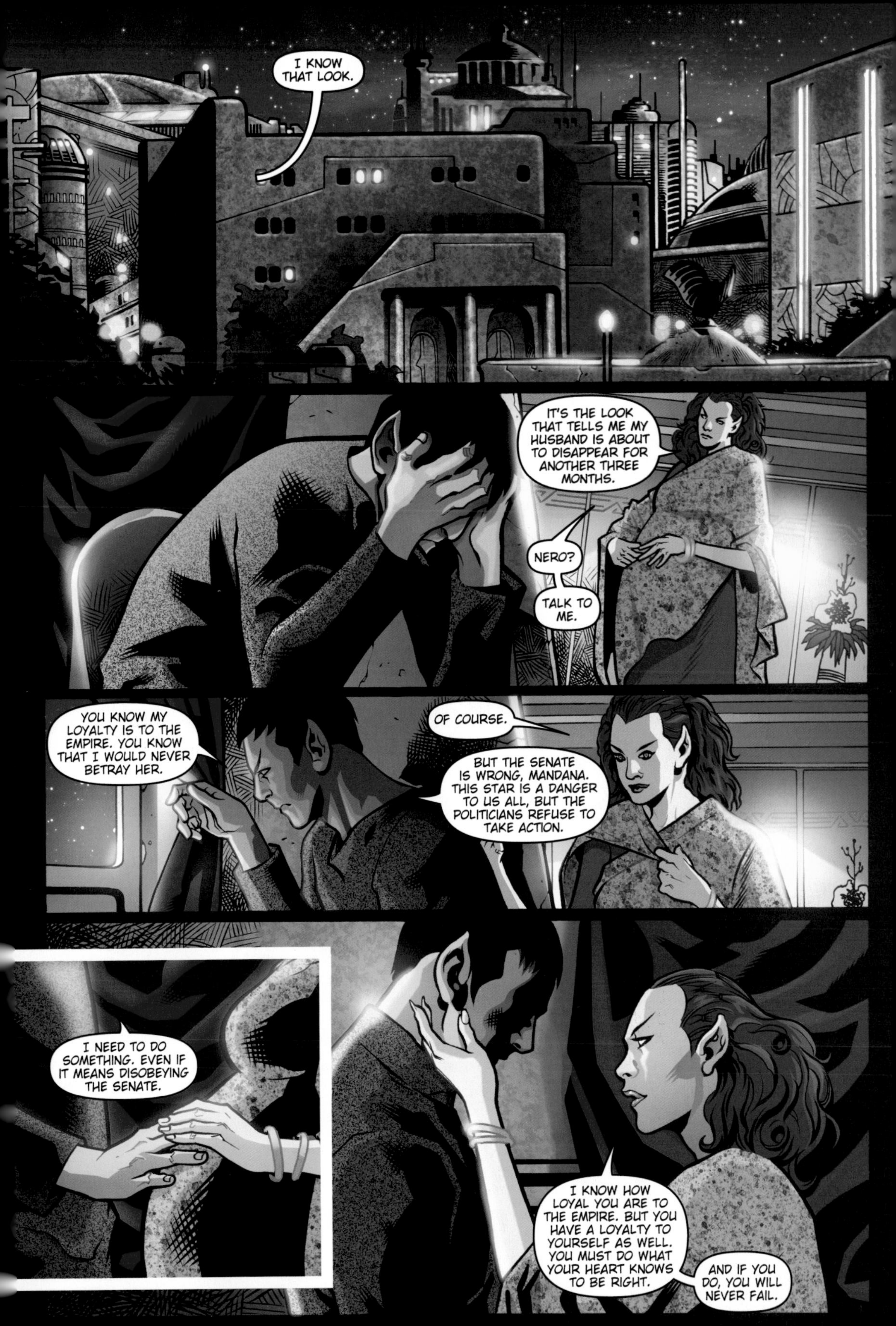
I KNOW THAT LOOK.
IT'S THE LOOK THAT TELLS ME MY HUSBAND IS ABOUT TO DISAPPEAR FOR ANOTHER THREE MONTHS.
NERO?
TALK TO ME.
YOU KNOW MY LOYALTY IS TO THE EMPIRE. YOU KNOW THAT I WOULD NEVER BETRAY HER.
OF COURSE.
BUT THE SENATE IS WRONG, MANDANA. THIS STAR IS A DANGER TO US ALL, BUT THE POLITICIANS REFUSE TO TAKE ACTION.
I NEED TO DO SOMETHING. EVEN IF IT MEANS DISOBEYING THE SENATE.
I KNOW HOW LOYAL YOU ARE TO THE EMPIRE. BUT YOU HAVE A LOYALTY TO YOURSELF AS WELL. YOU MUST DO WHAT YOUR HEART KNOWS TO BE RIGHT.
AND IF YOU DO, YOU WILL NEVER FAIL.

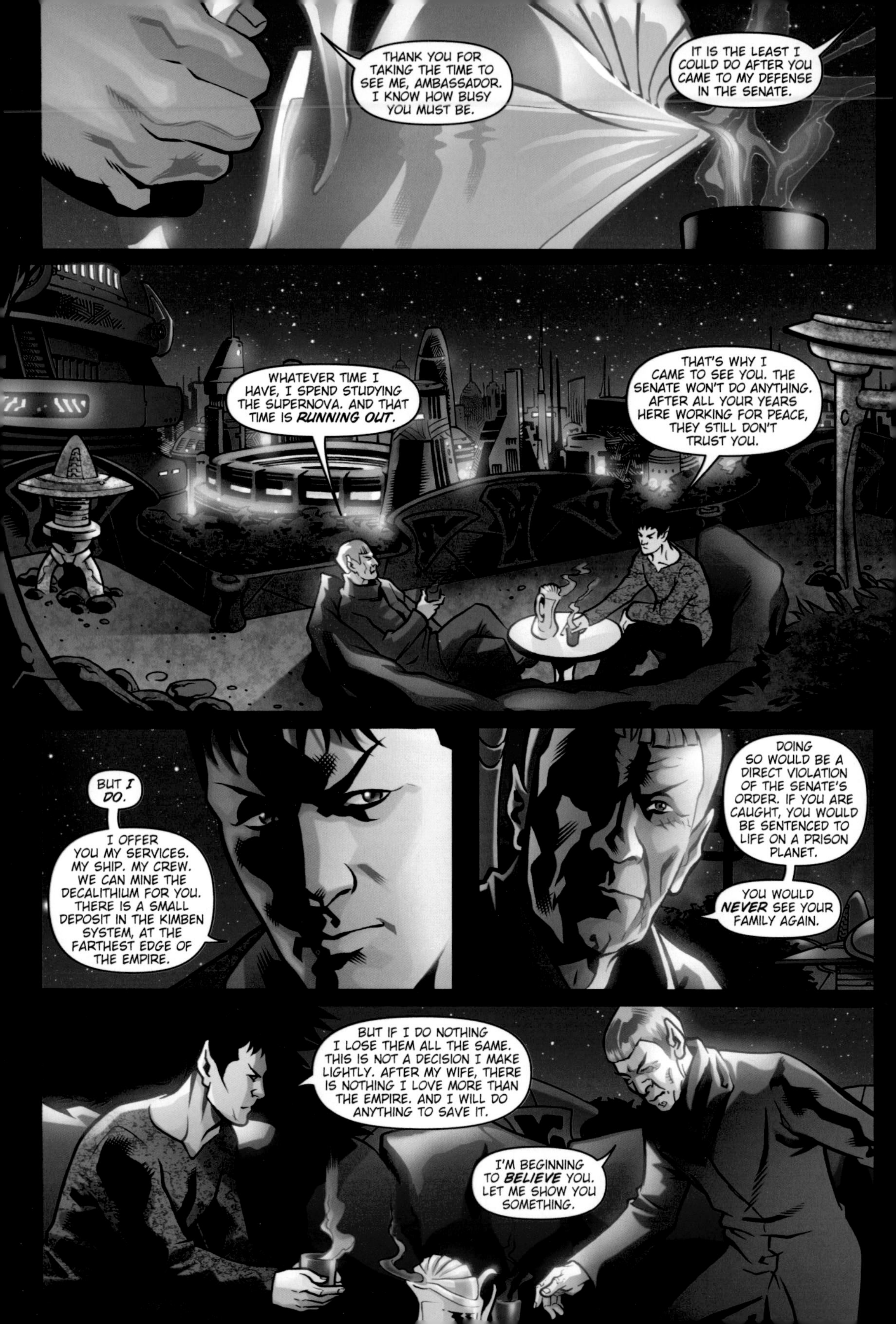
THANK YOU FOR TAKING THE TIME TO SEE ME, AMBASSADOR. I KNOW HOW BUSY YOU MUST BE.
IT IS THE LEAST I COULD DO AFTER YOU CAME TO MY DEFENSE IN THE SENATE.
WHATEVER TIME I HAVE, I SPEND STUDYING THE SUPERNOVA. AND THAT TIME IS **RUNNING OUT**.
THAT'S WHY I CAME TO SEE YOU. THE SENATE WON'T DO ANYTHING. AFTER ALL YOUR YEARS HERE WORKING FOR PEACE, THEY STILL DON'T TRUST YOU.
BUT ***I DO***.
I OFFER YOU MY SERVICES. MY SHIP. MY CREW. WE CAN MINE THE DECALITHIUM FOR YOU. THERE IS A SMALL DEPOSIT IN THE KIMBEN SYSTEM, AT THE FARTHEST EDGE OF THE EMPIRE.
DOING SO WOULD BE A DIRECT VIOLATION OF THE SENATE'S ORDER. IF YOU ARE CAUGHT, YOU WOULD BE SENTENCED TO LIFE ON A PRISON PLANET.
YOU WOULD **NEVER** SEE YOUR FAMILY AGAIN.
BUT IF I DO NOTHING I LOSE THEM ALL THE SAME. THIS IS NOT A DECISION I MAKE LIGHTLY. AFTER MY WIFE, THERE IS NOTHING I LOVE MORE THAN THE EMPIRE. AND I WILL DO ANYTHING TO SAVE IT.
I'M BEGINNING TO **BELIEVE** YOU. LET ME SHOW YOU SOMETHING.

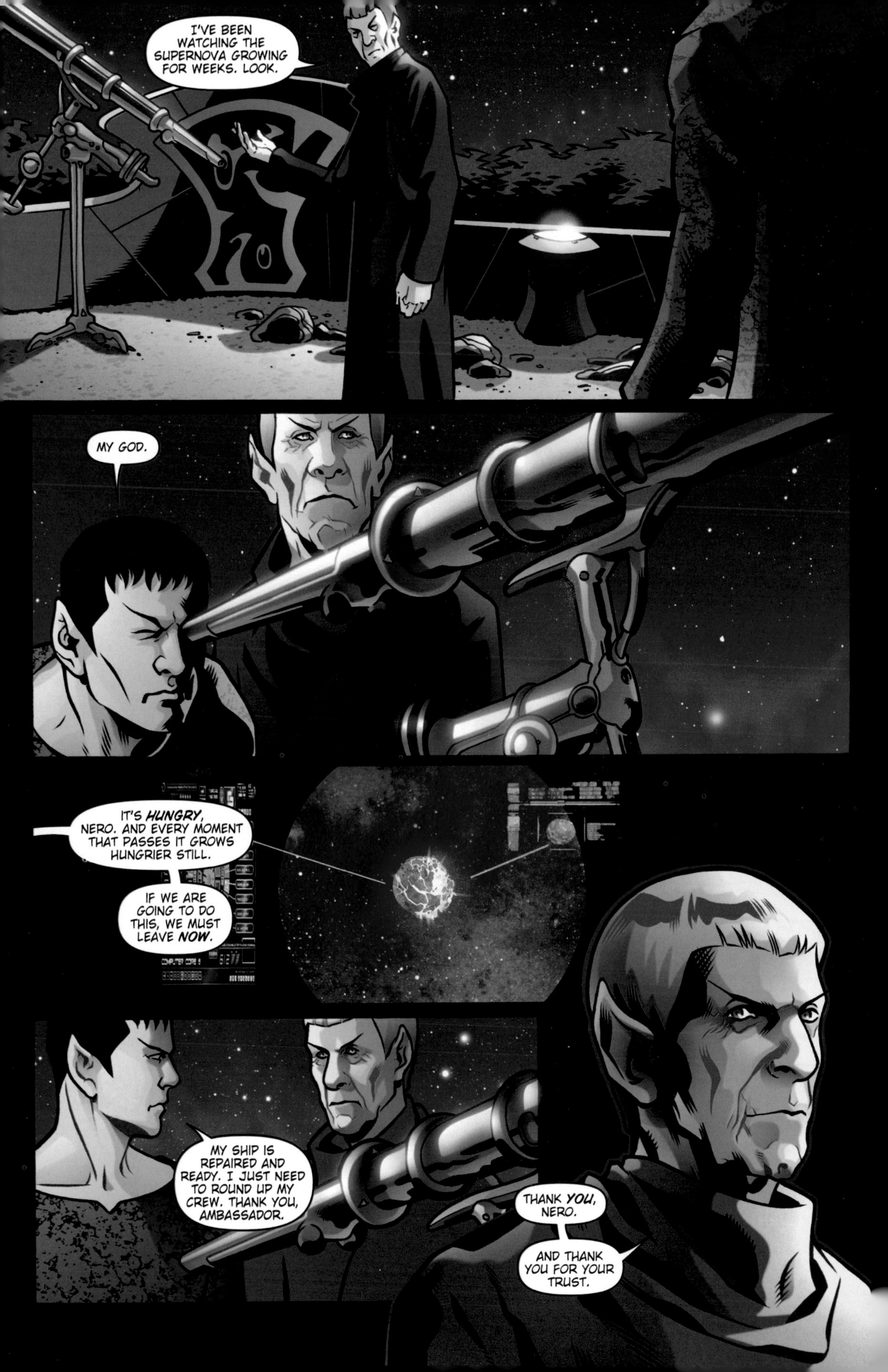
I'VE BEEN WATCHING THE SUPERNOVA GROWING FOR WEEKS. LOOK.
MY GOD.
IT'S *HUNGRY*, NERO. AND EVERY MOMENT THAT PASSES IT GROWS HUNGRIER STILL.
IF WE ARE GOING TO DO THIS, WE MUST LEAVE *NOW*.
MY SHIP IS REPAIRED AND READY. I JUST NEED TO ROUND UP MY CREW. THANK YOU, AMBASSADOR.
THANK *YOU*, NERO.
AND THANK YOU FOR YOUR TRUST.

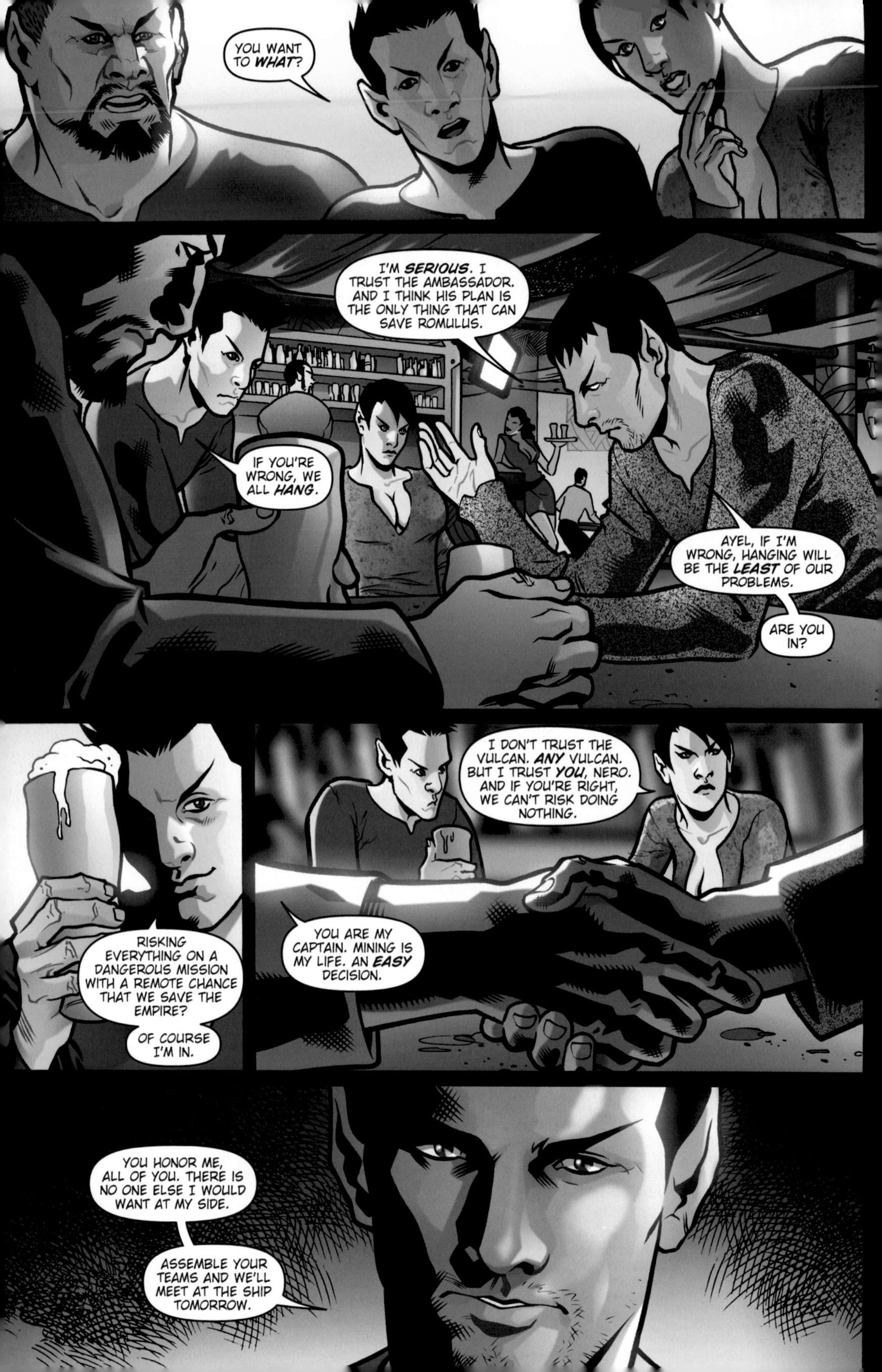

YOU WANT TO WHAT?
I'M SERIOUS. I TRUST THE AMBASSADOR. AND I THINK HIS PLAN IS THE ONLY THING THAT CAN SAVE ROMULUS.
IF YOU'RE WRONG, WE ALL HANG.
AYEL, IF I'M WRONG, HANGING WILL BE THE LEAST OF OUR PROBLEMS.
ARE YOU IN?
RISKING EVERYTHING ON A DANGEROUS MISSION WITH A REMOTE CHANCE THAT WE SAVE THE EMPIRE?
OF COURSE I'M IN.
I DON'T TRUST THE VULCAN. ANY VULCAN. BUT I TRUST YOU, NERO. AND IF YOU'RE RIGHT, WE CAN'T RISK DOING NOTHING.
YOU ARE MY CAPTAIN. MINING IS MY LIFE. AN EASY DECISION.
YOU HONOR ME, ALL OF YOU. THERE IS NO ONE ELSE I WOULD WANT AT MY SIDE.
ASSEMBLE YOUR TEAMS AND WE'LL MEET AT THE SHIP TOMORROW.

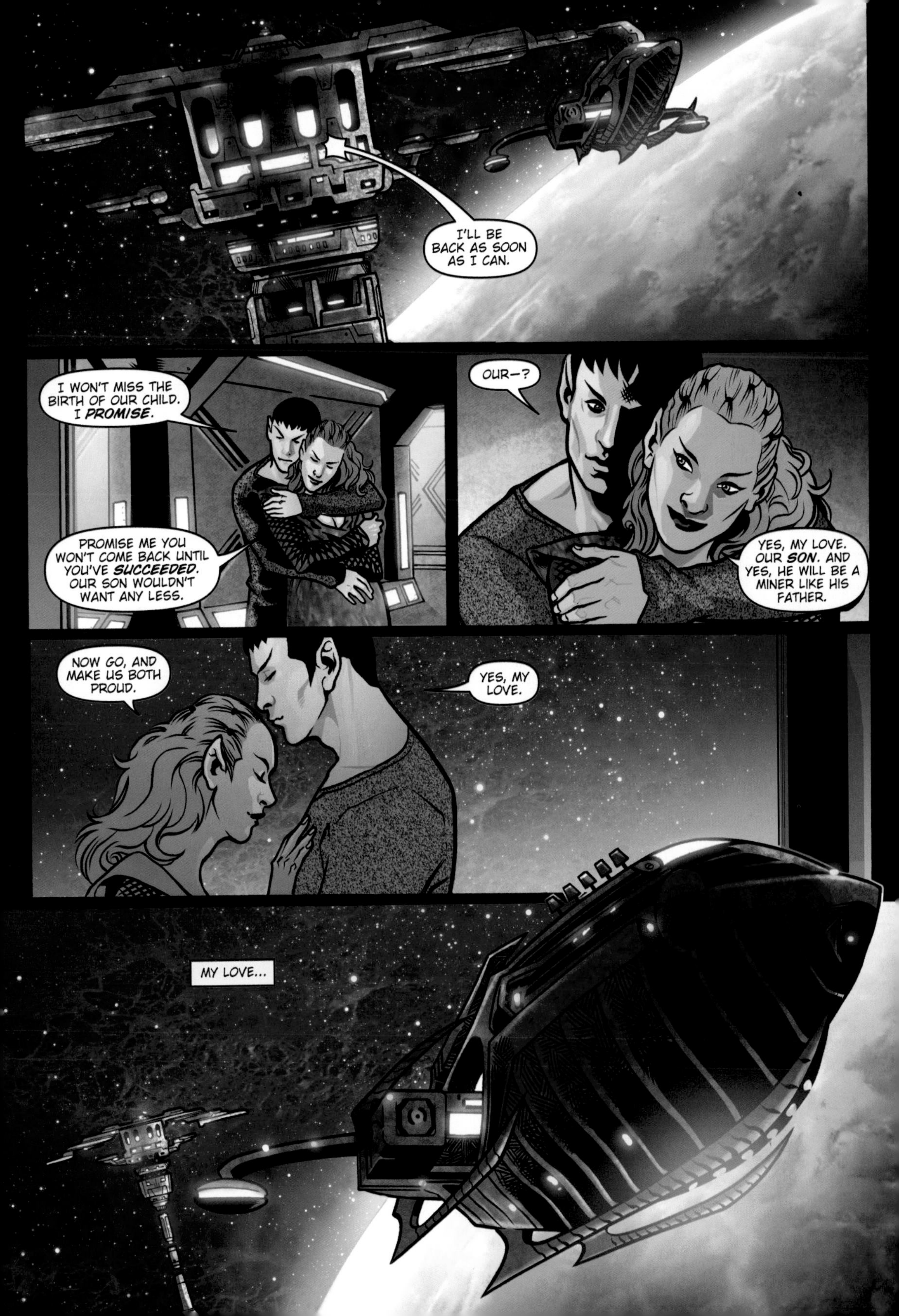
I'LL BE BACK AS SOON AS I CAN.
I WON'T MISS THE BIRTH OF OUR CHILD. I PROMISE.
PROMISE ME YOU WON'T COME BACK UNTIL YOU'VE SUCCEEDED. OUR SON WOULDN'T WANT ANY LESS.
OUR—?
YES, MY LOVE. OUR SON. AND YES, HE WILL BE A MINER LIKE HIS FATHER.
NOW GO, AND MAKE US BOTH PROUD.
YES, MY LOVE.
MY LOVE...

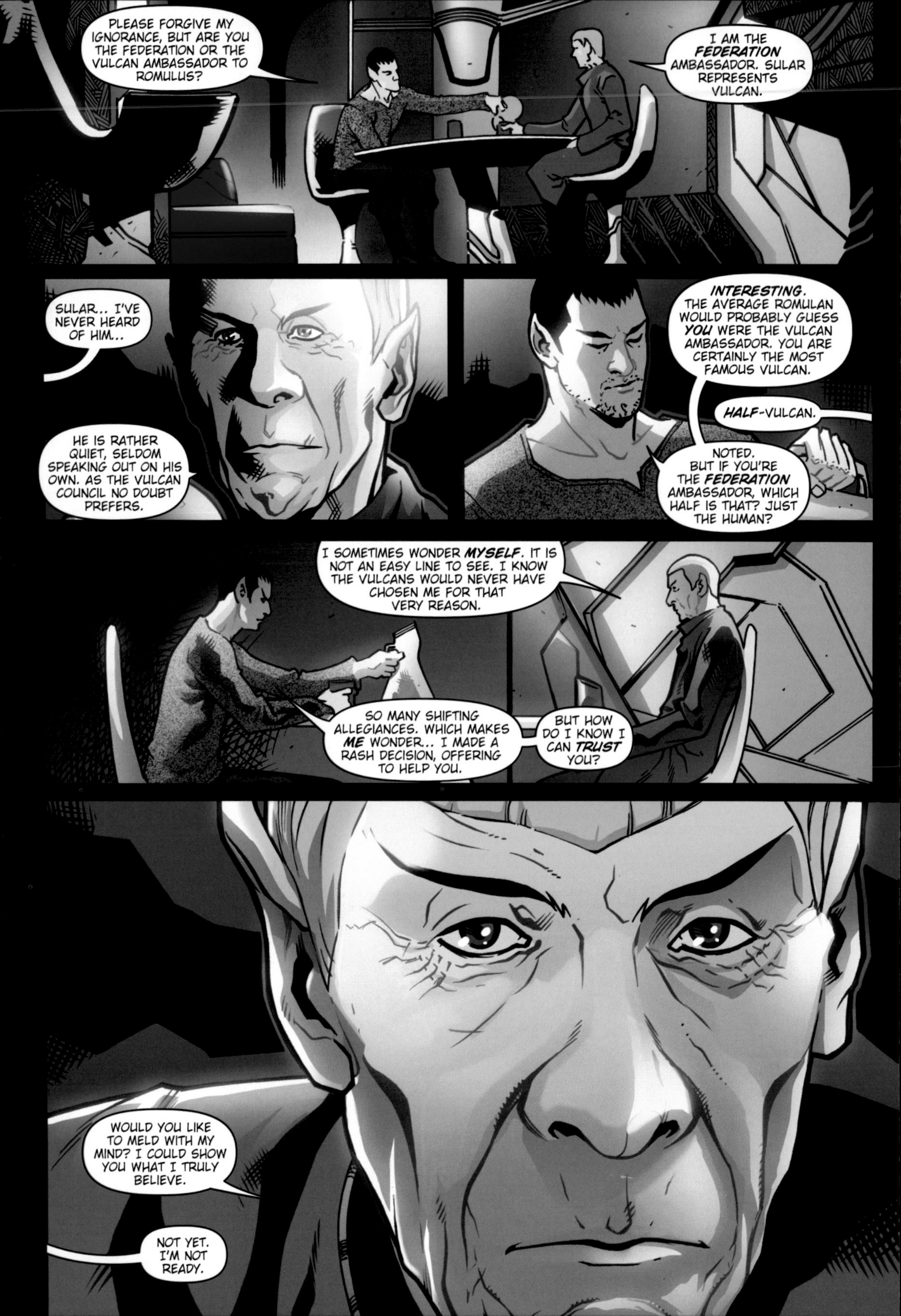
PLEASE FORGIVE MY IGNORANCE, BUT ARE YOU THE FEDERATION OR THE VULCAN AMBASSADOR TO ROMULUS?
I AM THE *FEDERATION* AMBASSADOR. SULAR REPRESENTS VULCAN.
SULAR... I'VE NEVER HEARD OF HIM...
HE IS RATHER QUIET, SELDOM SPEAKING OUT ON HIS OWN. AS THE VULCAN COUNCIL NO DOUBT PREFERS.
INTERESTING. THE AVERAGE ROMULAN WOULD PROBABLY GUESS *YOU* WERE THE VULCAN AMBASSADOR. YOU ARE CERTAINLY THE MOST FAMOUS VULCAN.
HALF-VULCAN.
NOTED. BUT IF YOU'RE THE *FEDERATION* AMBASSADOR, WHICH HALF IS THAT? JUST THE HUMAN?
I SOMETIMES WONDER *MYSELF*. IT IS NOT AN EASY LINE TO SEE. I KNOW THE VULCANS WOULD NEVER HAVE CHOSEN ME FOR THAT VERY REASON.
SO MANY SHIFTING ALLEGIANCES. WHICH MAKES *ME* WONDER... I MADE A RASH DECISION, OFFERING TO HELP YOU.
BUT HOW DO I KNOW I CAN *TRUST* YOU?
WOULD YOU LIKE TO MELD WITH MY MIND? I COULD SHOW YOU WHAT I TRULY BELIEVE.
NOT YET. I'M NOT READY.

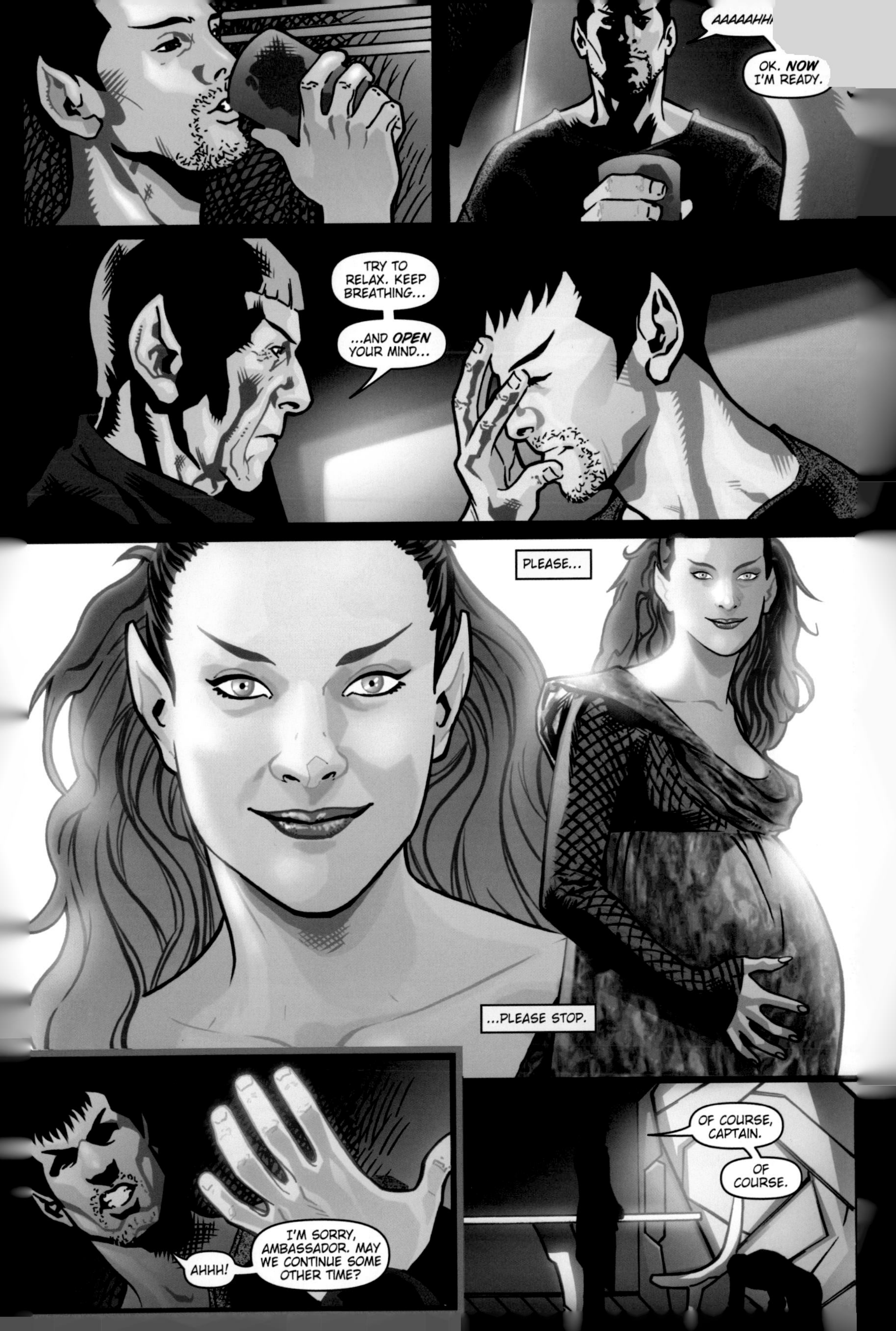
AAAAAHH!
OK. NOW I'M READY.
TRY TO RELAX. KEEP BREATHING...
...AND OPEN YOUR MIND...
PLEASE...
...PLEASE STOP.
AHHH!
I'M SORRY, AMBASSADOR. MAY WE CONTINUE SOME OTHER TIME?
OF COURSE, CAPTAIN.
OF COURSE.

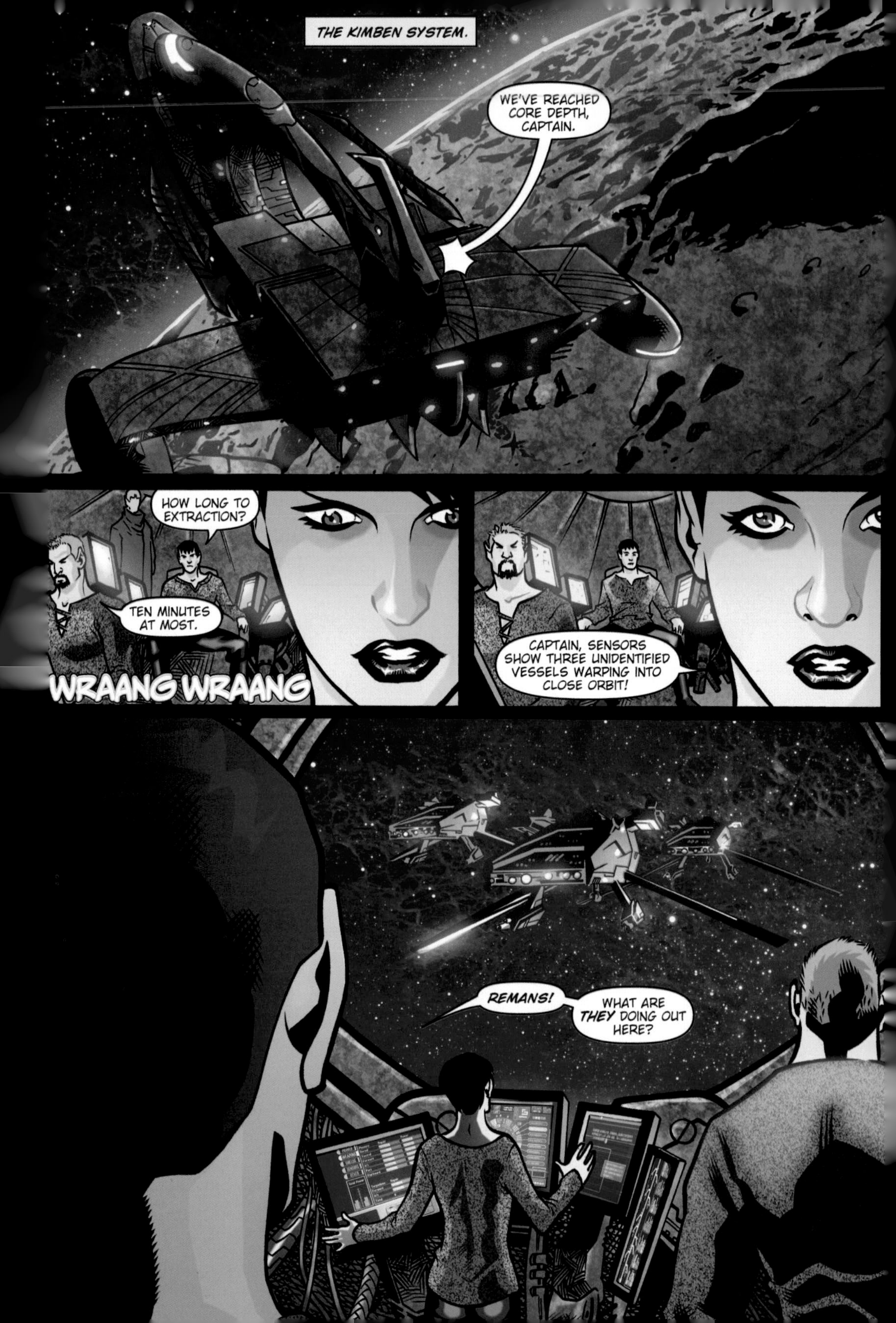

THE KIMBEN SYSTEM.
WE'VE REACHED CORE DEPTH, CAPTAIN.
HOW LONG TO EXTRACTION?
TEN MINUTES AT MOST.
WRAANG WRAANG
CAPTAIN, SENSORS SHOW THREE UNIDENTIFIED VESSELS WARPING INTO CLOSE ORBIT!
REMANS!
WHAT ARE THEY DOING OUT HERE?

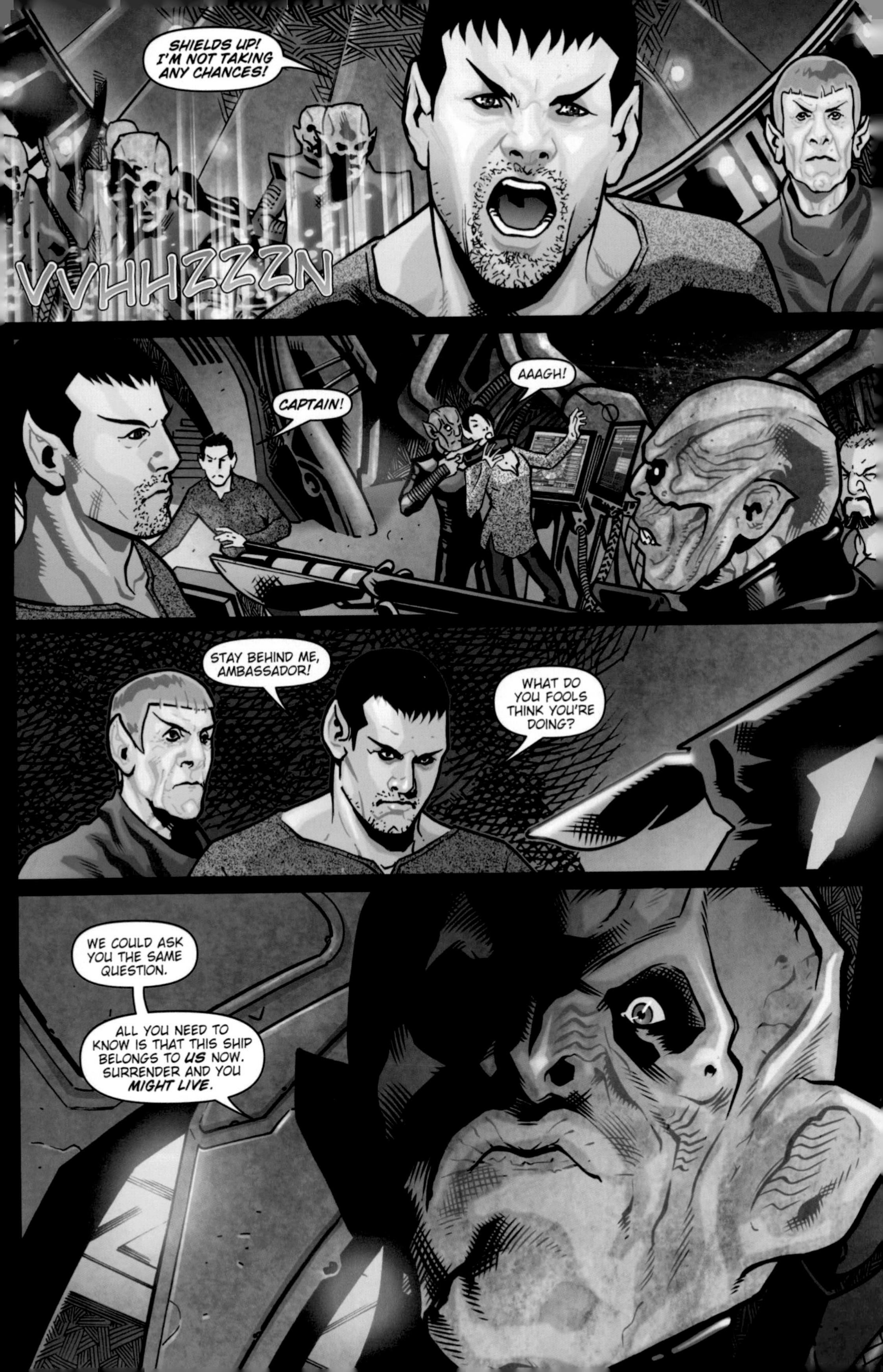
SHIELDS UP! I'M NOT TAKING ANY CHANCES!
VVHHZZZN
CAPTAIN!
AAAGH!
STAY BEHIND ME, AMBASSADOR!
WHAT DO YOU FOOLS THINK YOU'RE DOING?
WE COULD ASK YOU THE SAME QUESTION.
ALL YOU NEED TO KNOW IS THAT THIS SHIP BELONGS TO US NOW. SURRENDER AND YOU MIGHT LIVE.

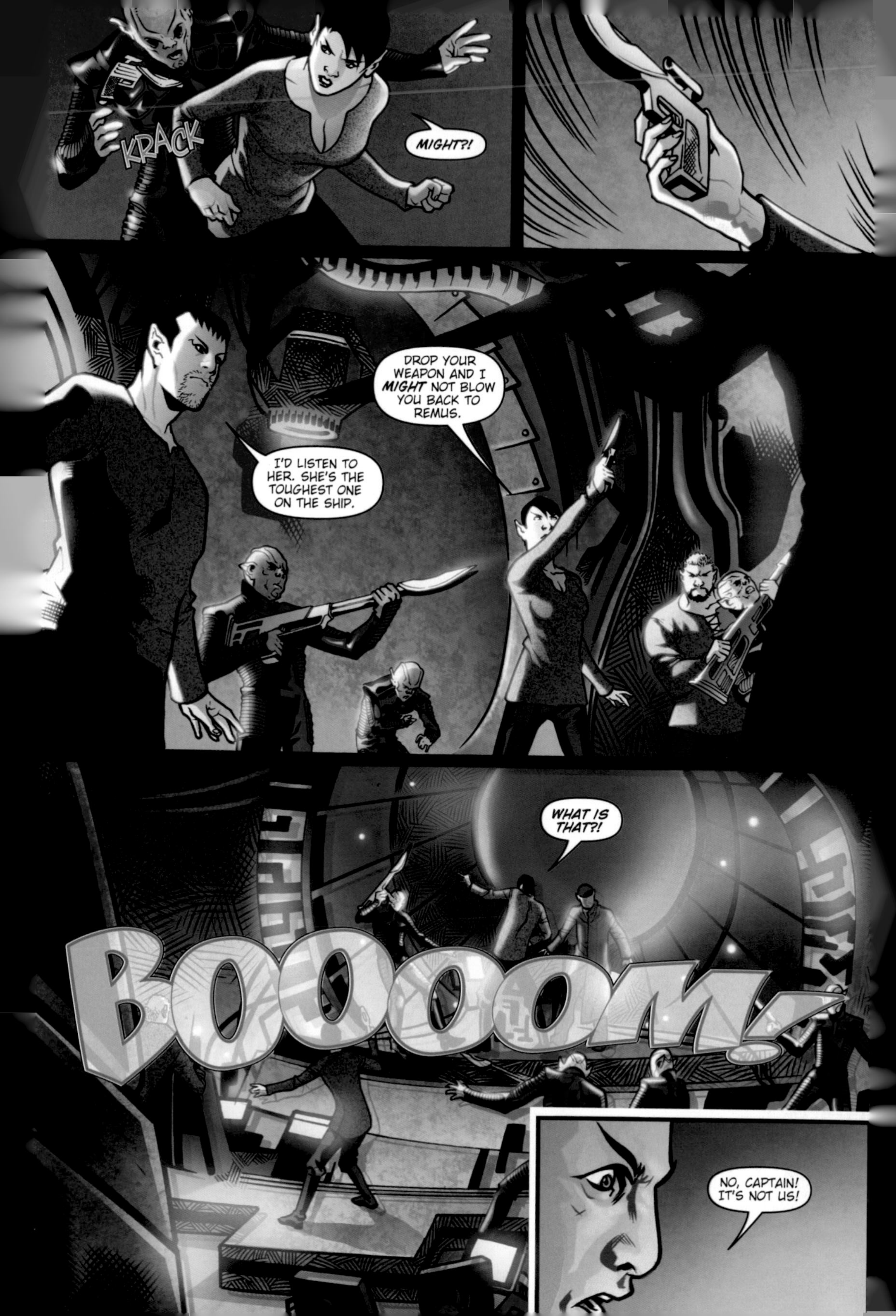
KRACK
MIGHT?!
DROP YOUR WEAPON AND I MIGHT NOT BLOW YOU BACK TO REMUS.
I'D LISTEN TO HER. SHE'S THE TOUGHEST ONE ON THE SHIP.
WHAT IS THAT?!
BOOOOM!
NO, CAPTAIN! IT'S NOT US!

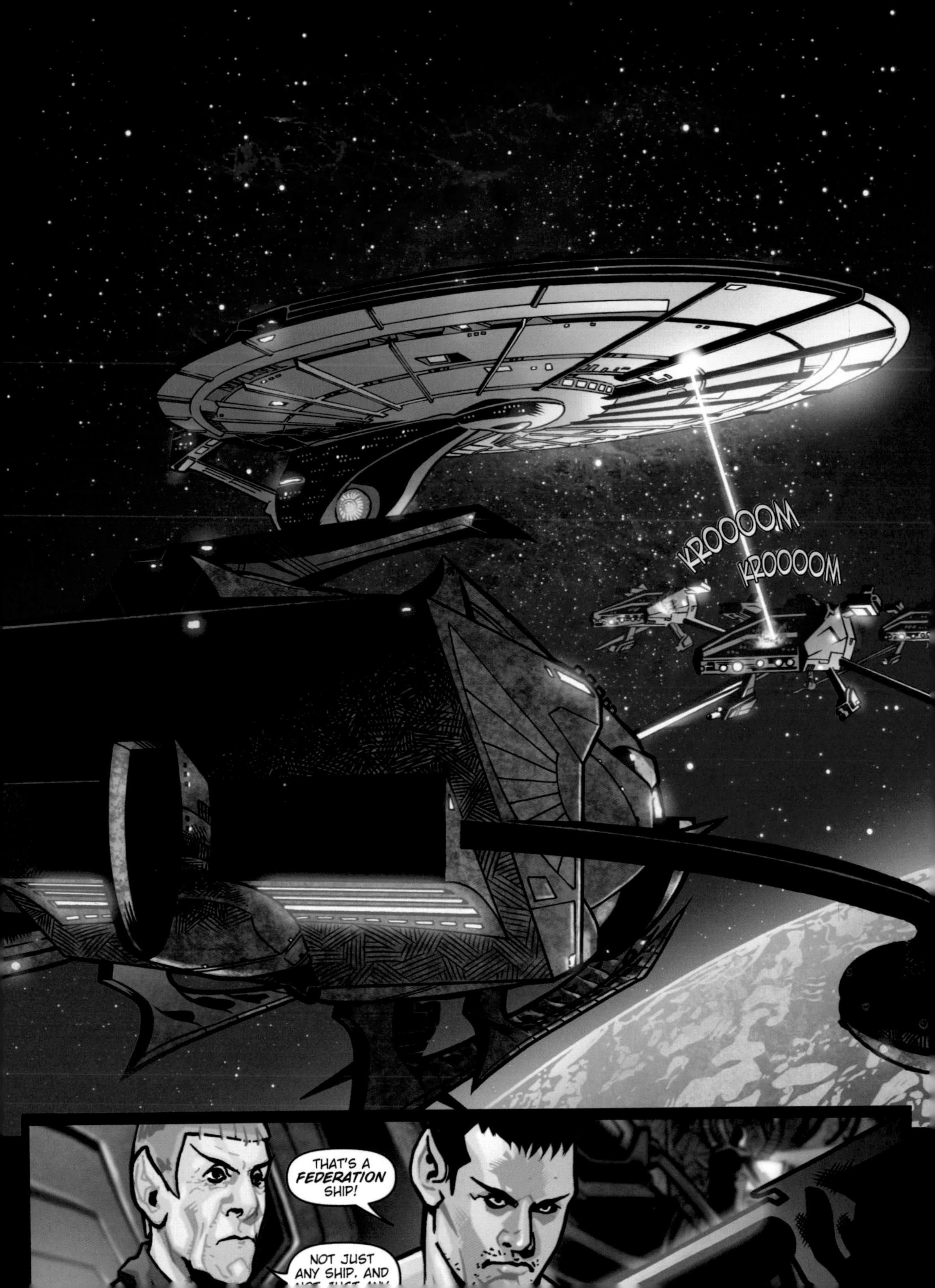
KROOOOM
KROOOOM
THAT'S A FEDERATION SHIP!
NOT JUST ANY SHIP. AND

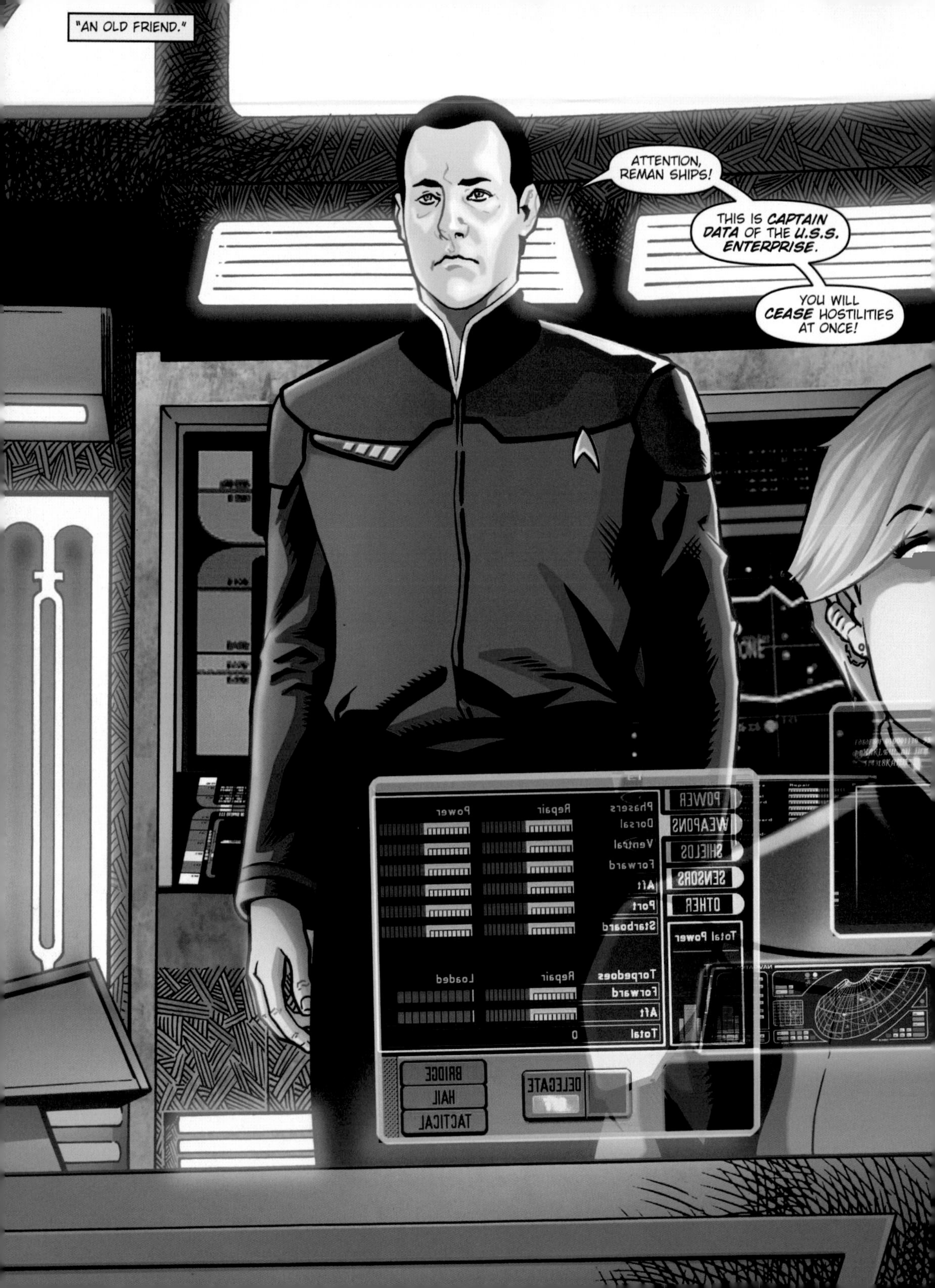
"AN OLD FRIEND."
ATTENTION, REMAN SHIPS!
THIS IS CAPTAIN DATA OF THE U.S.S. ENTERPRISE.
YOU WILL CEASE HOSTILITIES AT ONCE!

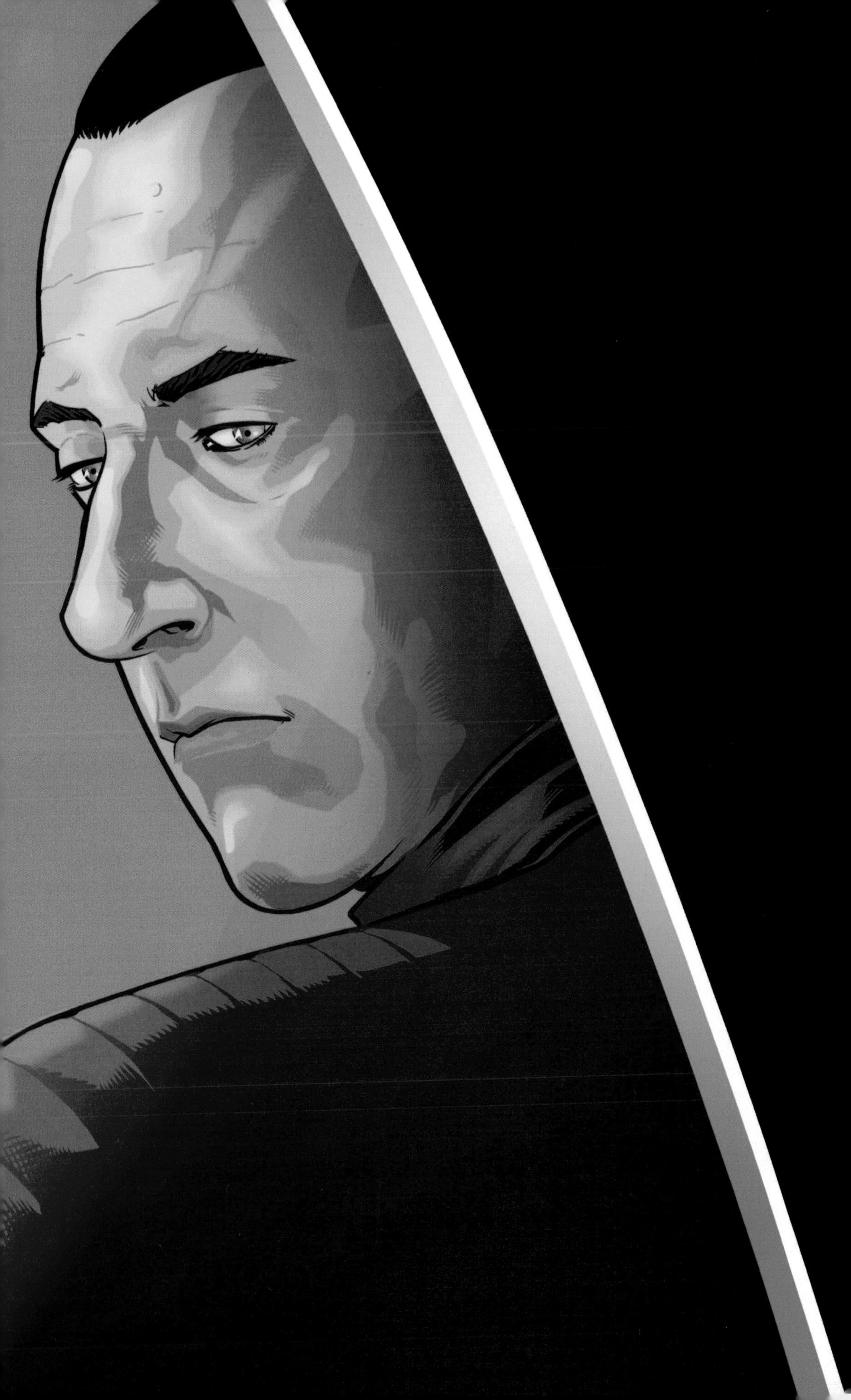

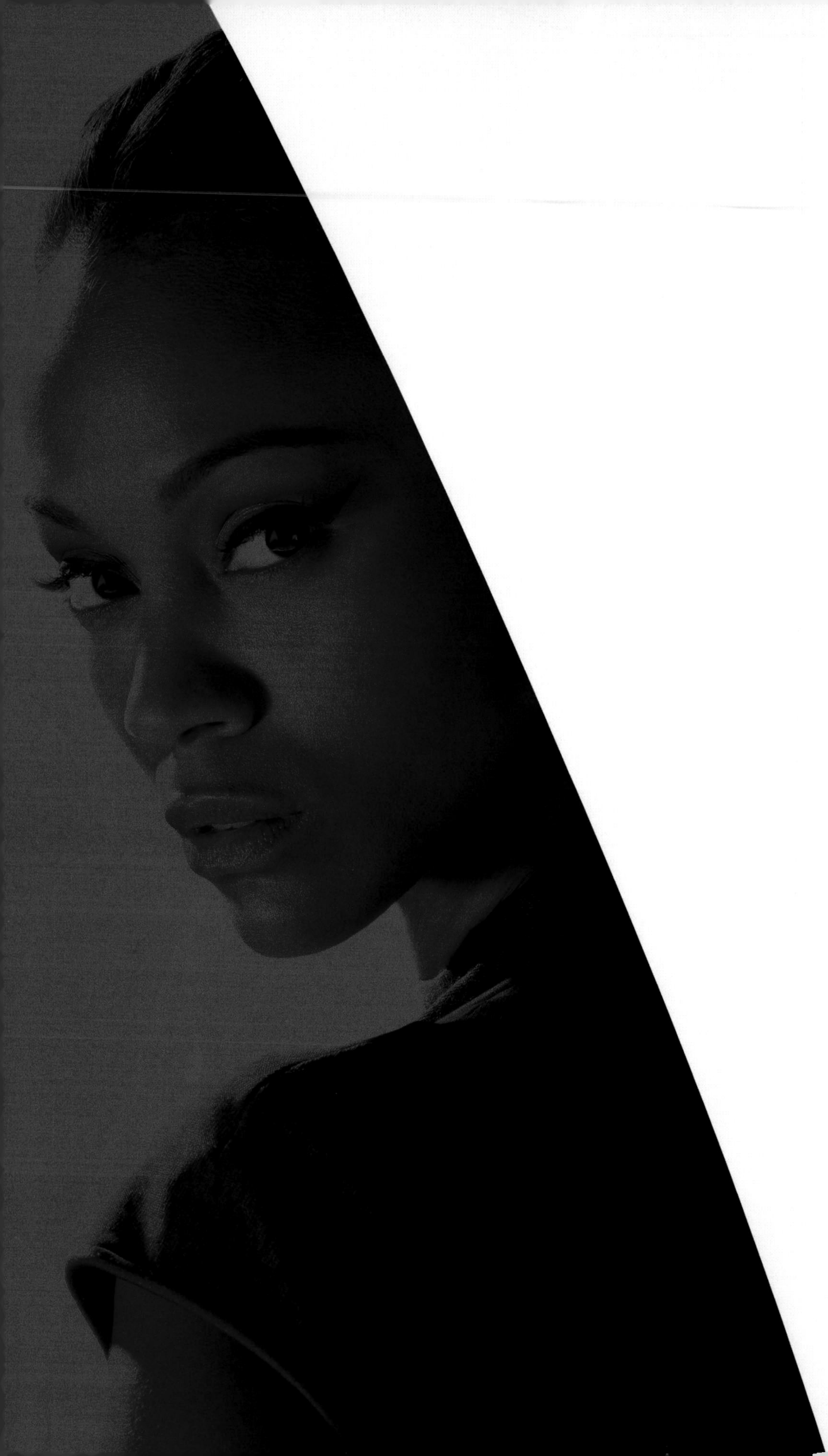

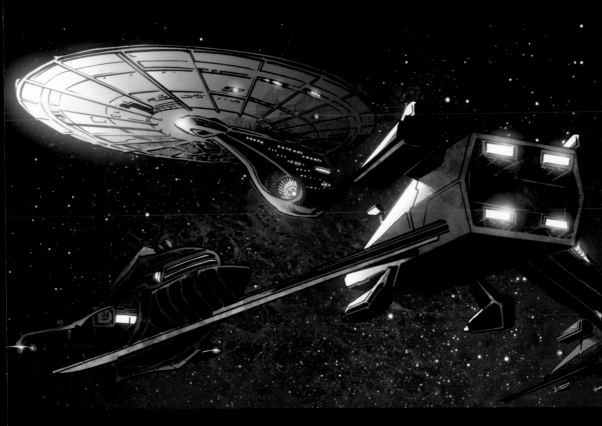

STARDATE 64390.1

DEEPER IN ROMULAN
TERRITORY...

WHERE ONLY A FEW HAVE
GONE BEFORE...

STAR TREK

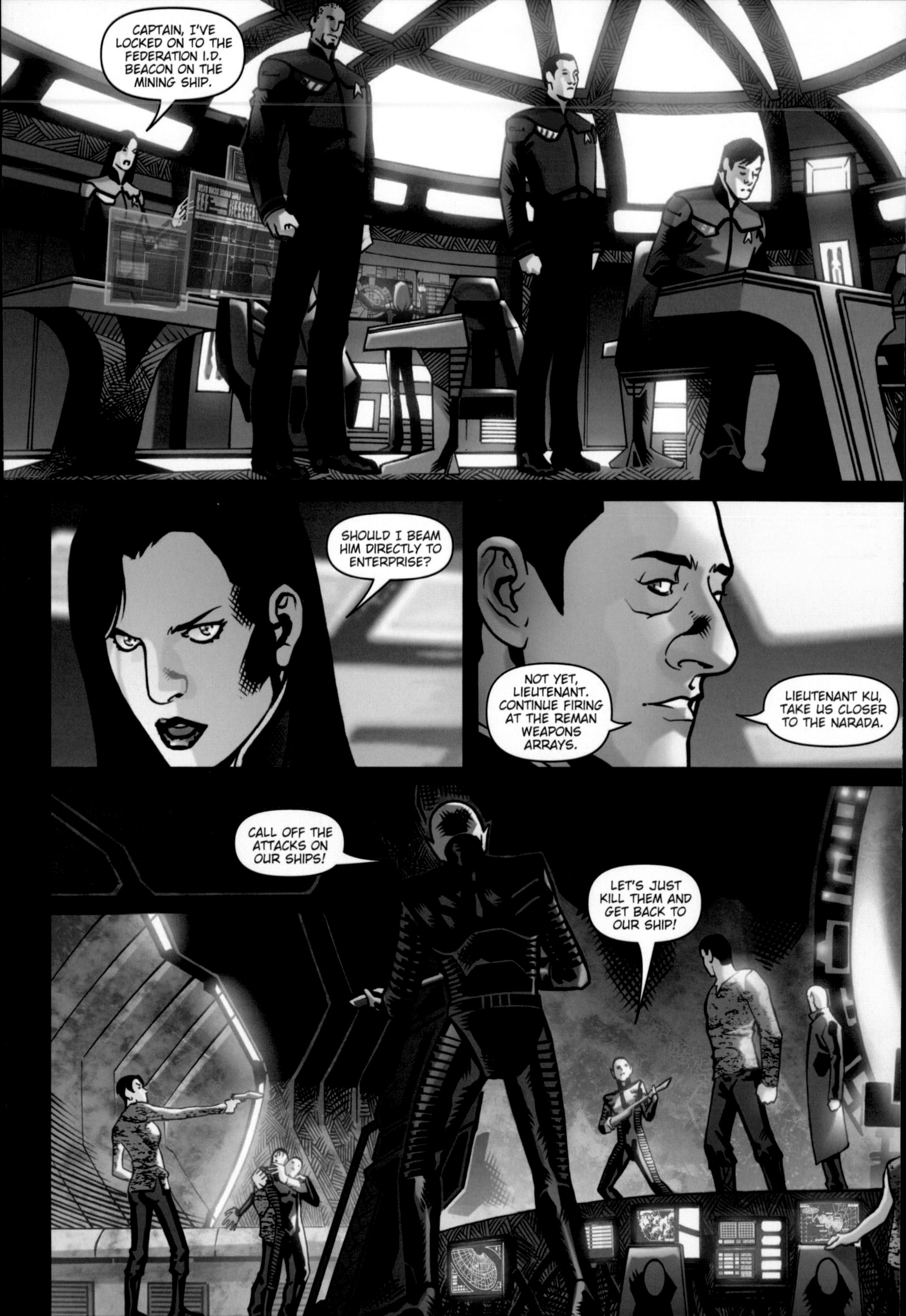
CAPTAIN, I'VE LOCKED ON TO THE FEDERATION I.D. BEACON ON THE MINING SHIP.
SHOULD I BEAM HIM DIRECTLY TO ENTERPRISE?
NOT YET, LIEUTENANT. CONTINUE FIRING AT THE REMAN WEAPONS ARRAYS.
LIEUTENANT KU, TAKE US CLOSER TO THE NARADA.
CALL OFF THE ATTACKS ON OUR SHIPS!
LET'S JUST KILL THEM AND GET BACK TO OUR SHIP!

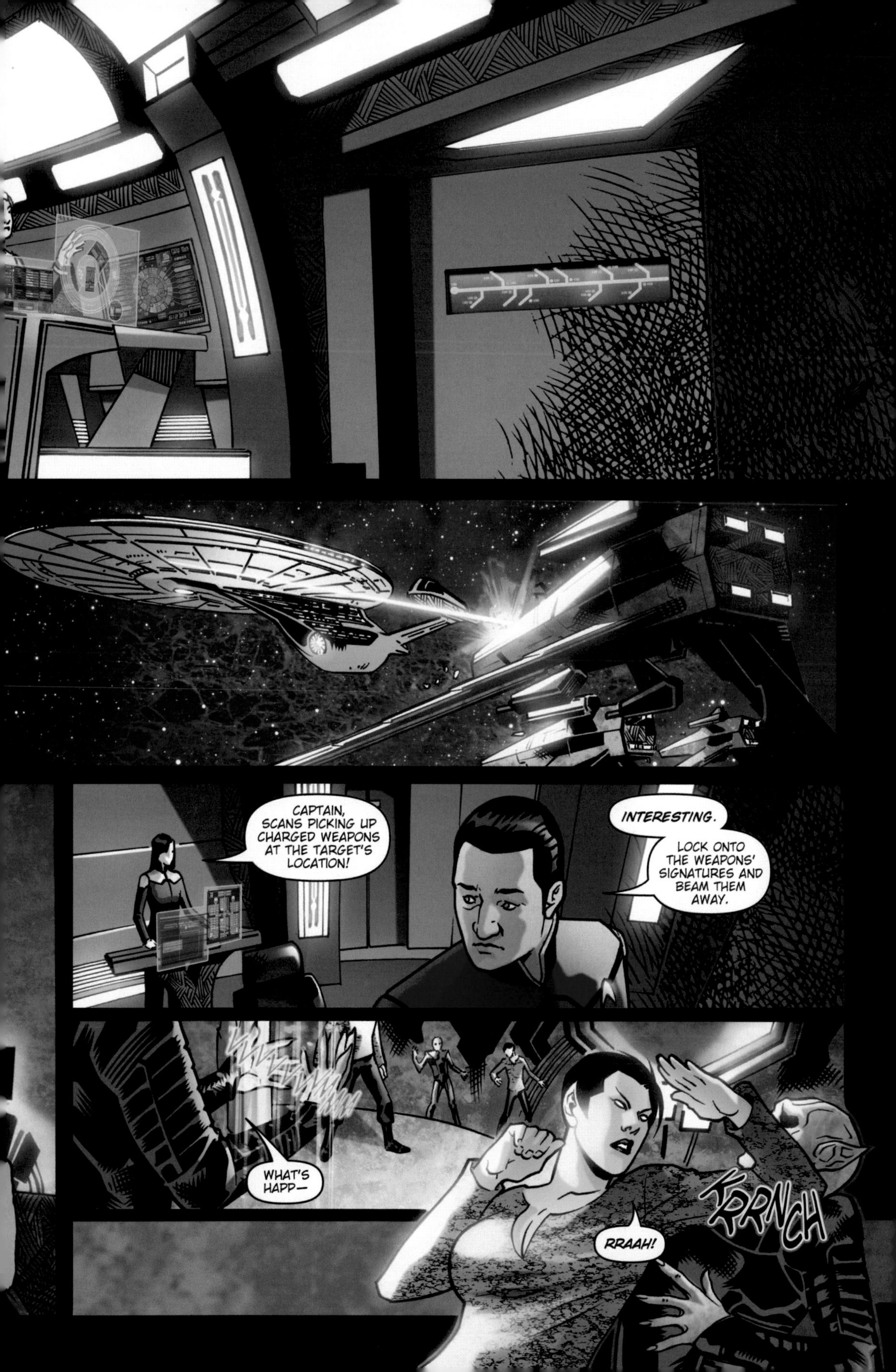
CAPTAIN, SCANS PICKING UP CHARGED WEAPONS AT THE TARGET'S LOCATION!
INTERESTING.
LOCK ONTO THE WEAPONS' SIGNATURES AND BEAM THEM AWAY.
WHAT'S HAPP—
RRAAH!
KRRNCH

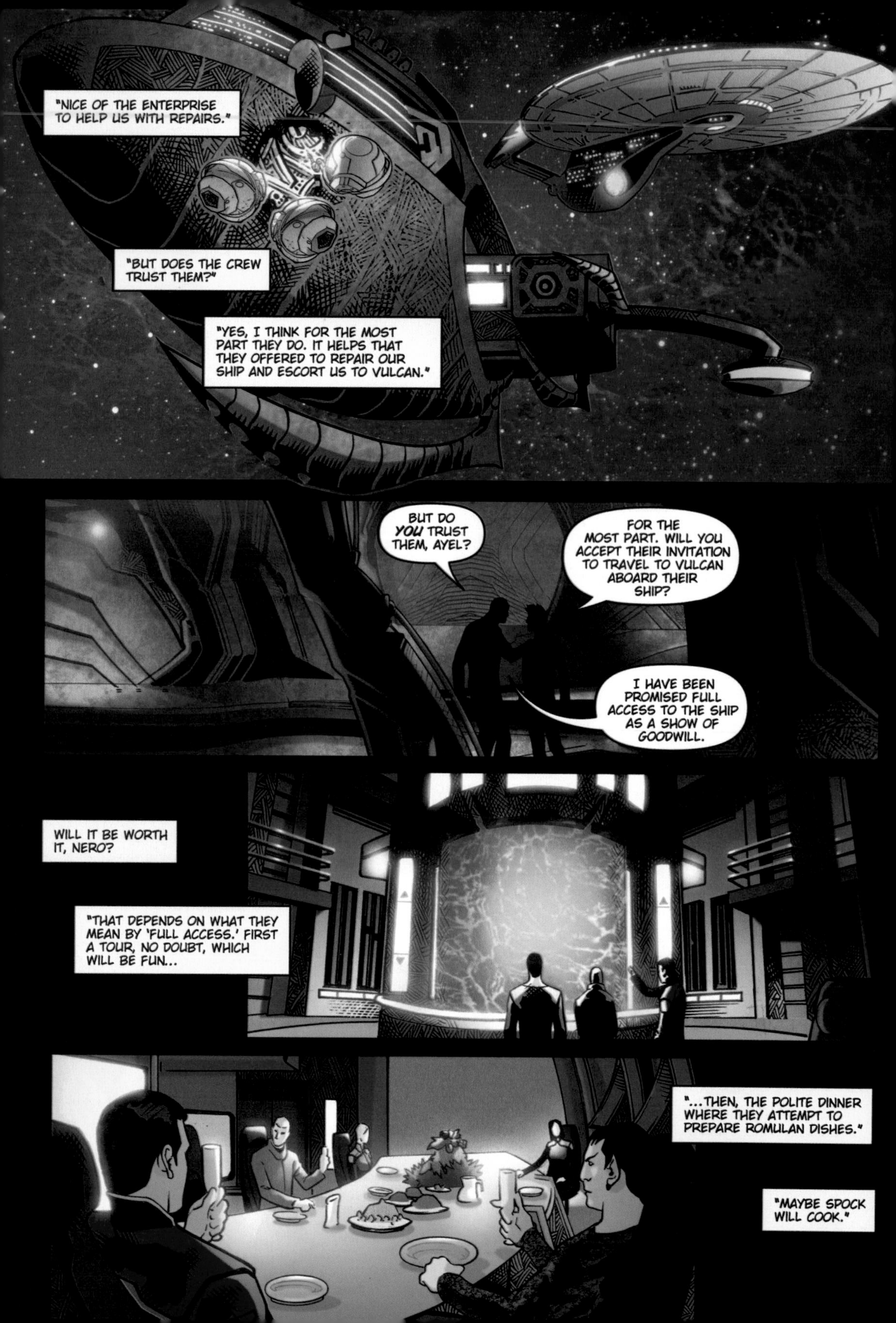
"NICE OF THE ENTERPRISE TO HELP US WITH REPAIRS."
"BUT DOES THE CREW TRUST THEM?"
"YES, I THINK FOR THE MOST PART THEY DO. IT HELPS THAT THEY OFFERED TO REPAIR OUR SHIP AND ESCORT US TO VULCAN."
BUT DO *YOU* TRUST THEM, AYEL?
FOR THE MOST PART. WILL YOU ACCEPT THEIR INVITATION TO TRAVEL TO VULCAN ABOARD THEIR SHIP?
I HAVE BEEN PROMISED FULL ACCESS TO THE SHIP AS A SHOW OF GOODWILL.
WILL IT BE WORTH IT, NERO?
"THAT DEPENDS ON WHAT THEY MEAN BY 'FULL ACCESS.' FIRST A TOUR, NO DOUBT, WHICH WILL BE FUN...
"...THEN, THE POLITE DINNER WHERE THEY ATTEMPT TO PREPARE ROMULAN DISHES."
"MAYBE SPOCK WILL COOK."

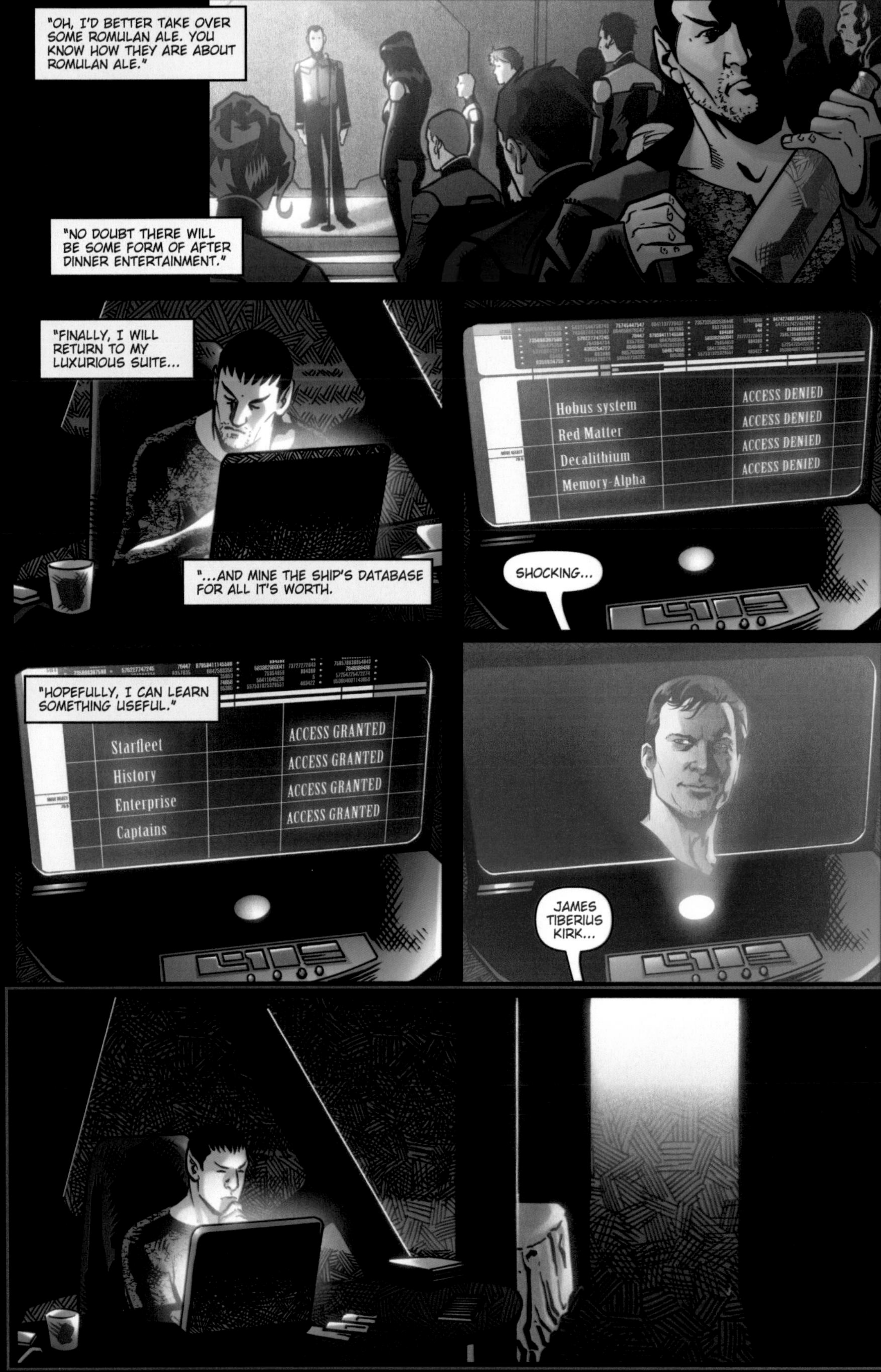
"OH, I'D BETTER TAKE OVER SOME ROMULAN ALE. YOU KNOW HOW THEY ARE ABOUT ROMULAN ALE."
"NO DOUBT THERE WILL BE SOME FORM OF AFTER DINNER ENTERTAINMENT."
"FINALLY, I WILL RETURN TO MY LUXURIOUS SUITE...
"...AND MINE THE SHIP'S DATABASE FOR ALL IT'S WORTH.
Hobus system
ACCESS DENIED
Red Matter
ACCESS DENIED
Decalithium
ACCESS DENIED
Memory-Alpha
ACCESS DENIED
SHOCKING...
"HOPEFULLY, I CAN LEARN SOMETHING USEFUL."
Starfleet
ACCESS GRANTED
History
ACCESS GRANTED
Enterprise
ACCESS GRANTED
Captains
ACCESS GRANTED
JAMES TIBERIUS KIRK...

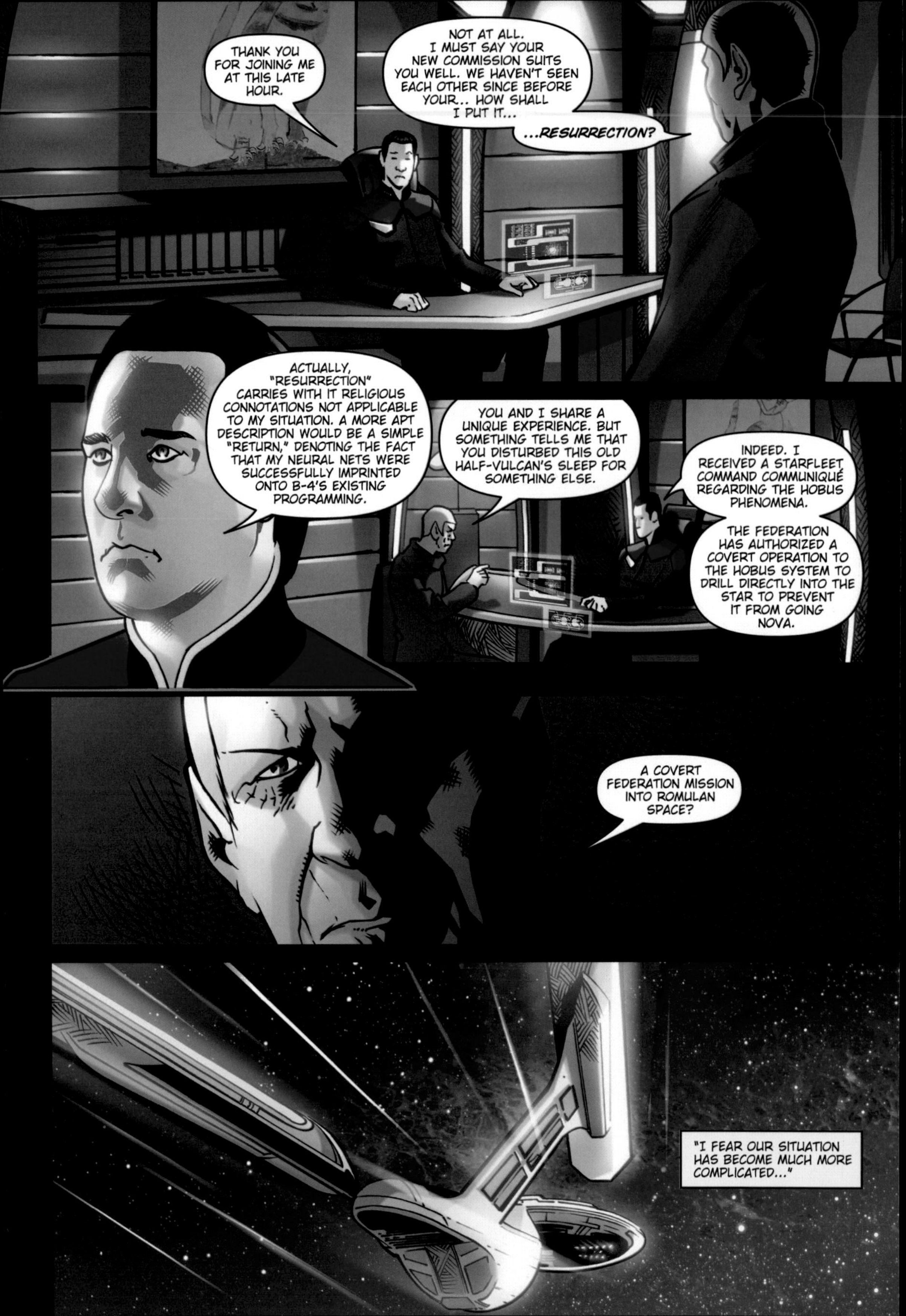
THANK YOU FOR JOINING ME AT THIS LATE HOUR.
NOT AT ALL. I MUST SAY YOUR NEW COMMISSION SUITS YOU WELL. WE HAVEN'T SEEN EACH OTHER SINCE BEFORE YOUR... HOW SHALL I PUT IT...
...RESURRECTION?
ACTUALLY, "RESURRECTION" CARRIES WITH IT RELIGIOUS CONNOTATIONS NOT APPLICABLE TO MY SITUATION. A MORE APT DESCRIPTION WOULD BE A SIMPLE "RETURN," DENOTING THE FACT THAT MY NEURAL NETS WERE SUCCESSFULLY IMPRINTED ONTO B-4'S EXISTING PROGRAMMING.
YOU AND I SHARE A UNIQUE EXPERIENCE. BUT SOMETHING TELLS ME THAT YOU DISTURBED THIS OLD HALF-VULCAN'S SLEEP FOR SOMETHING ELSE.
INDEED. I RECEIVED A STARFLEET COMMAND COMMUNIQUÉ REGARDING THE HOBUS PHENOMENA.
THE FEDERATION HAS AUTHORIZED A COVERT OPERATION TO THE HOBUS SYSTEM TO DRILL DIRECTLY INTO THE STAR TO PREVENT IT FROM GOING NOVA.
A COVERT FEDERATION MISSION INTO ROMULAN SPACE?
"I FEAR OUR SITUATION HAS BECOME MUCH MORE COMPLICATED..."

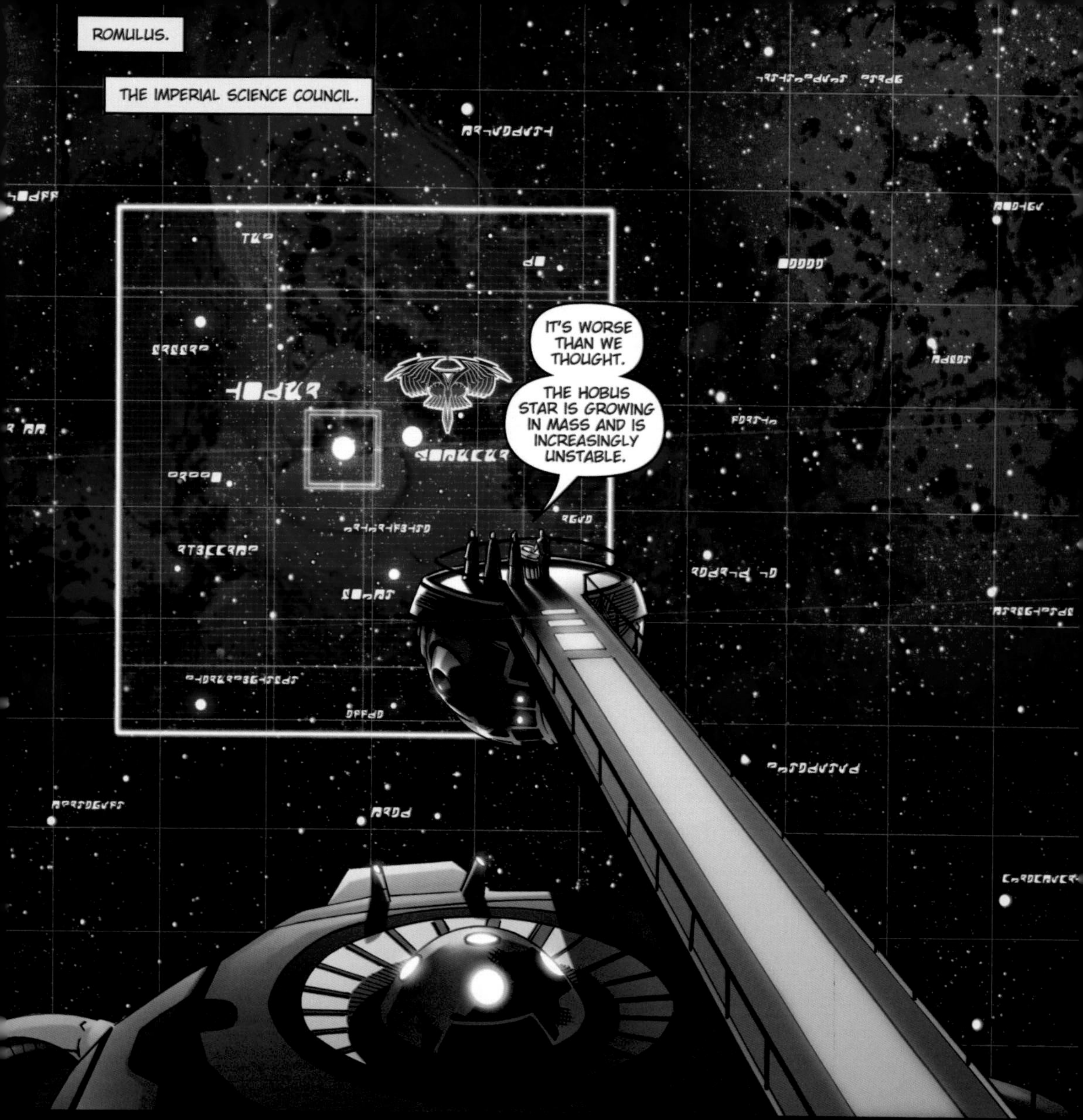
ROMULUS.
THE IMPERIAL SCIENCE COUNCIL.
IT'S WORSE THAN WE THOUGHT.
THE HOBUS STAR IS GROWING IN MASS AND IS INCREASINGLY UNSTABLE.

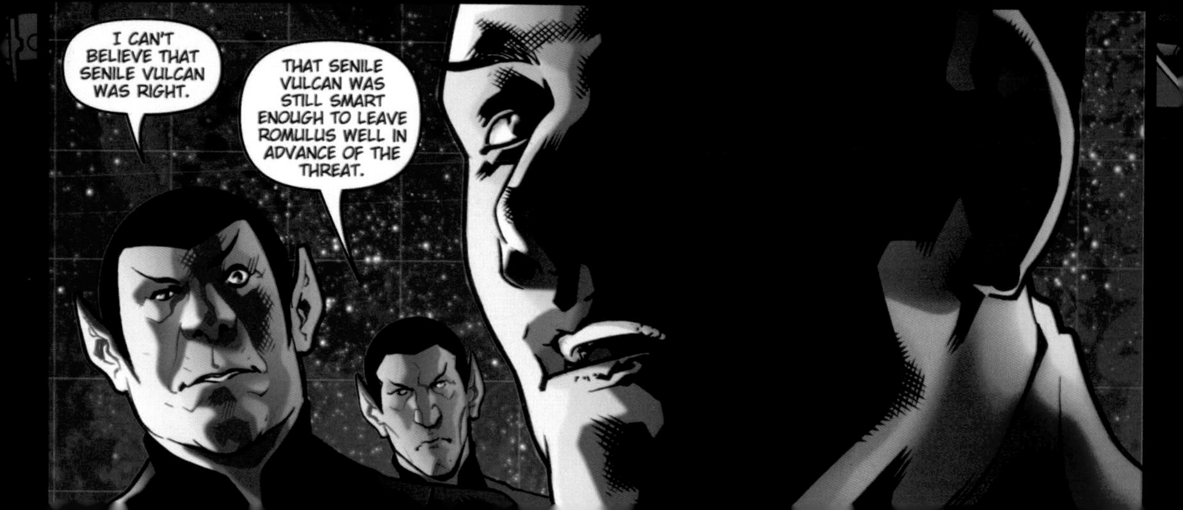
I CAN'T BELIEVE THAT SENILE VULCAN WAS RIGHT.
THAT SENILE VULCAN WAS STILL SMART ENOUGH TO LEAVE ROMULUS WELL IN ADVANCE OF THE THREAT.

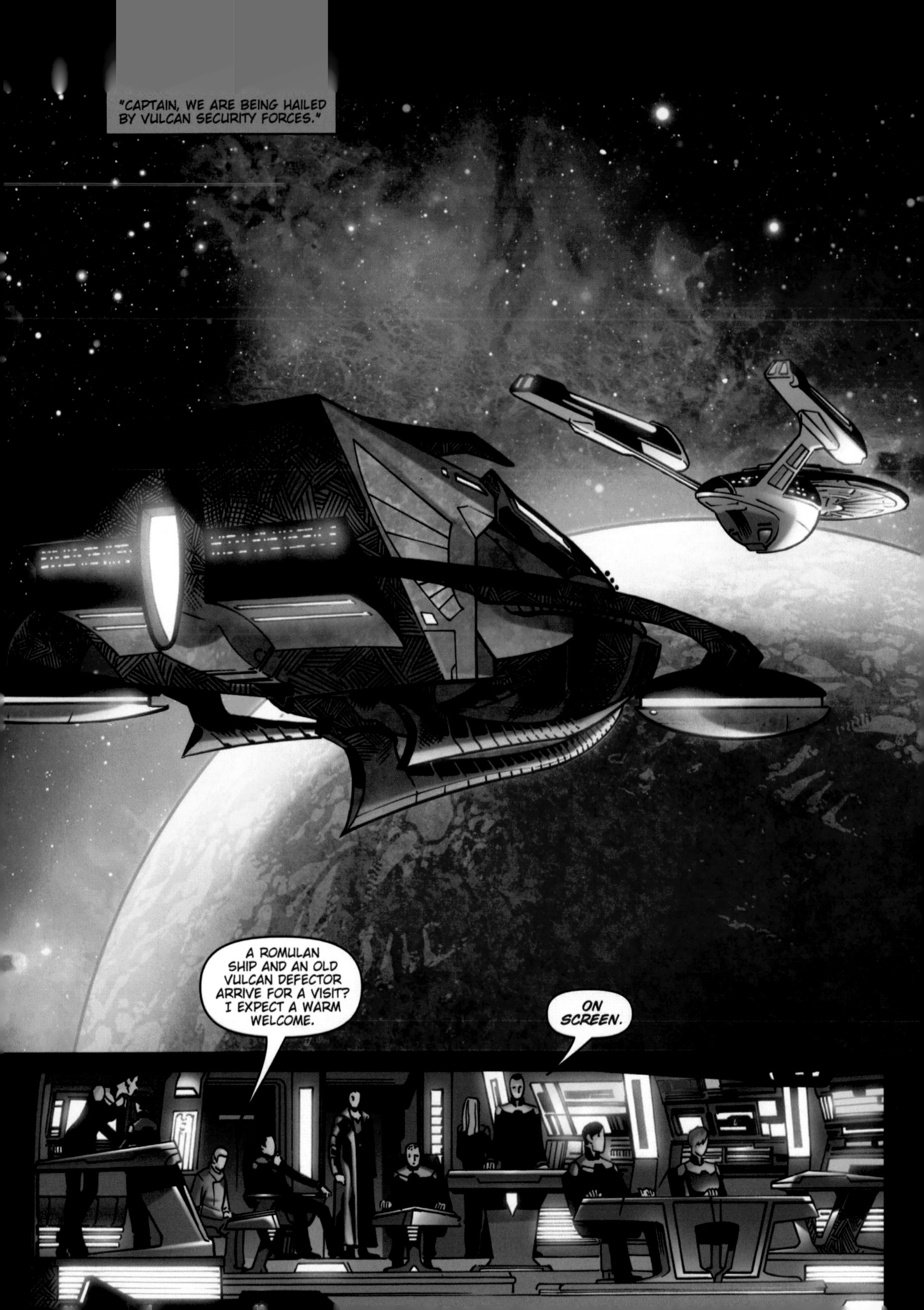
"CAPTAIN, WE ARE BEING HAILED BY VULCAN SECURITY FORCES."
A ROMULAN SHIP AND AN OLD VULCAN DEFECTOR ARRIVE FOR A VISIT? I EXPECT A WARM WELCOME.
ON SCREEN.

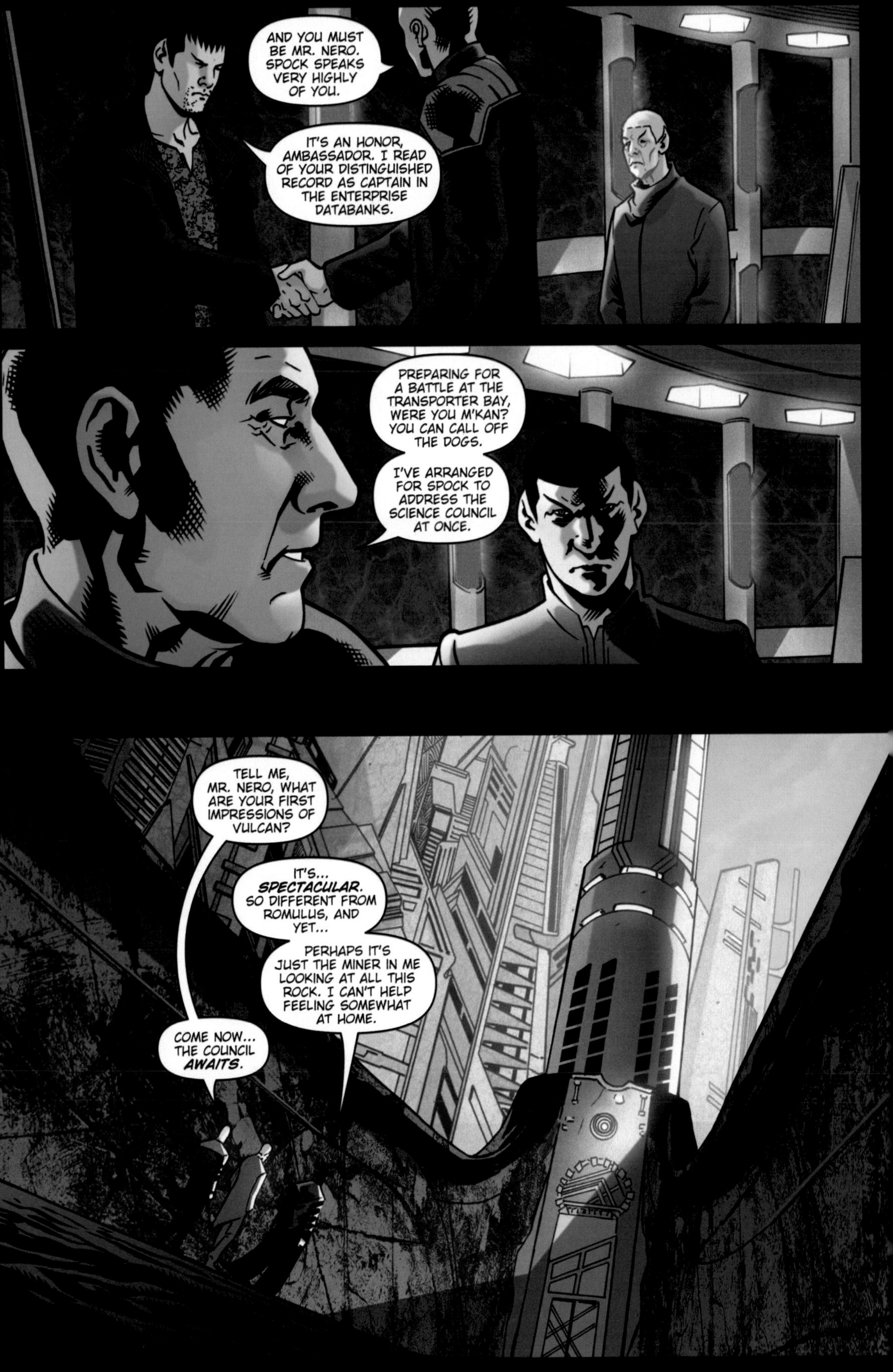
AND YOU MUST BE MR. NERO. SPOCK SPEAKS VERY HIGHLY OF YOU.
IT'S AN HONOR, AMBASSADOR. I READ OF YOUR DISTINGUISHED RECORD AS CAPTAIN IN THE ENTERPRISE DATABANKS.
PREPARING FOR A BATTLE AT THE TRANSPORTER BAY, WERE YOU M'KAN? YOU CAN CALL OFF THE DOGS.
I'VE ARRANGED FOR SPOCK TO ADDRESS THE SCIENCE COUNCIL AT ONCE.
TELL ME, MR. NERO, WHAT ARE YOUR FIRST IMPRESSIONS OF VULCAN?
IT'S... SPECTACULAR. SO DIFFERENT FROM ROMULUS, AND YET...
PERHAPS IT'S JUST THE MINER IN ME LOOKING AT ALL THIS ROCK. I CAN'T HELP FEELING SOMEWHAT AT HOME.
COME NOW... THE COUNCIL AWAITS.

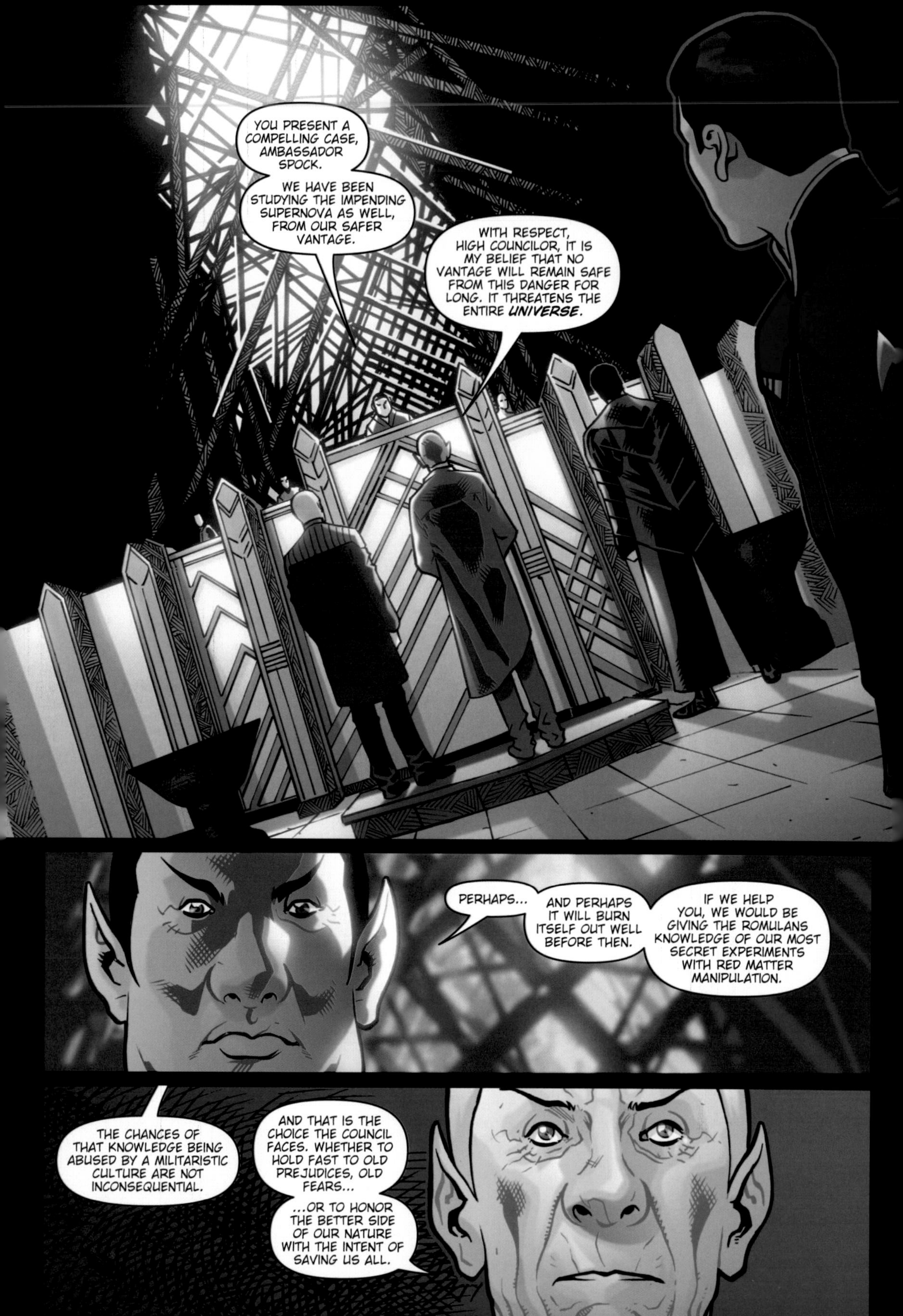
YOU PRESENT A COMPELLING CASE, AMBASSADOR SPOCK.
WE HAVE BEEN STUDYING THE IMPENDING SUPERNOVA AS WELL, FROM OUR SAFER VANTAGE.
WITH RESPECT, HIGH COUNCILOR, IT IS MY BELIEF THAT NO VANTAGE WILL REMAIN SAFE FROM THIS DANGER FOR LONG. IT THREATENS THE ENTIRE *UNIVERSE*.
PERHAPS...
AND PERHAPS IT WILL BURN ITSELF OUT WELL BEFORE THEN.
IF WE HELP YOU, WE WOULD BE GIVING THE ROMULANS KNOWLEDGE OF OUR MOST SECRET EXPERIMENTS WITH RED MATTER MANIPULATION.
THE CHANCES OF THAT KNOWLEDGE BEING ABUSED BY A MILITARISTIC CULTURE ARE NOT INCONSEQUENTIAL.
AND THAT IS THE CHOICE THE COUNCIL FACES. WHETHER TO HOLD FAST TO OLD PREJUDICES, OLD FEARS...
...OR TO HONOR THE BETTER SIDE OF OUR NATURE WITH THE INTENT OF SAVING US ALL.

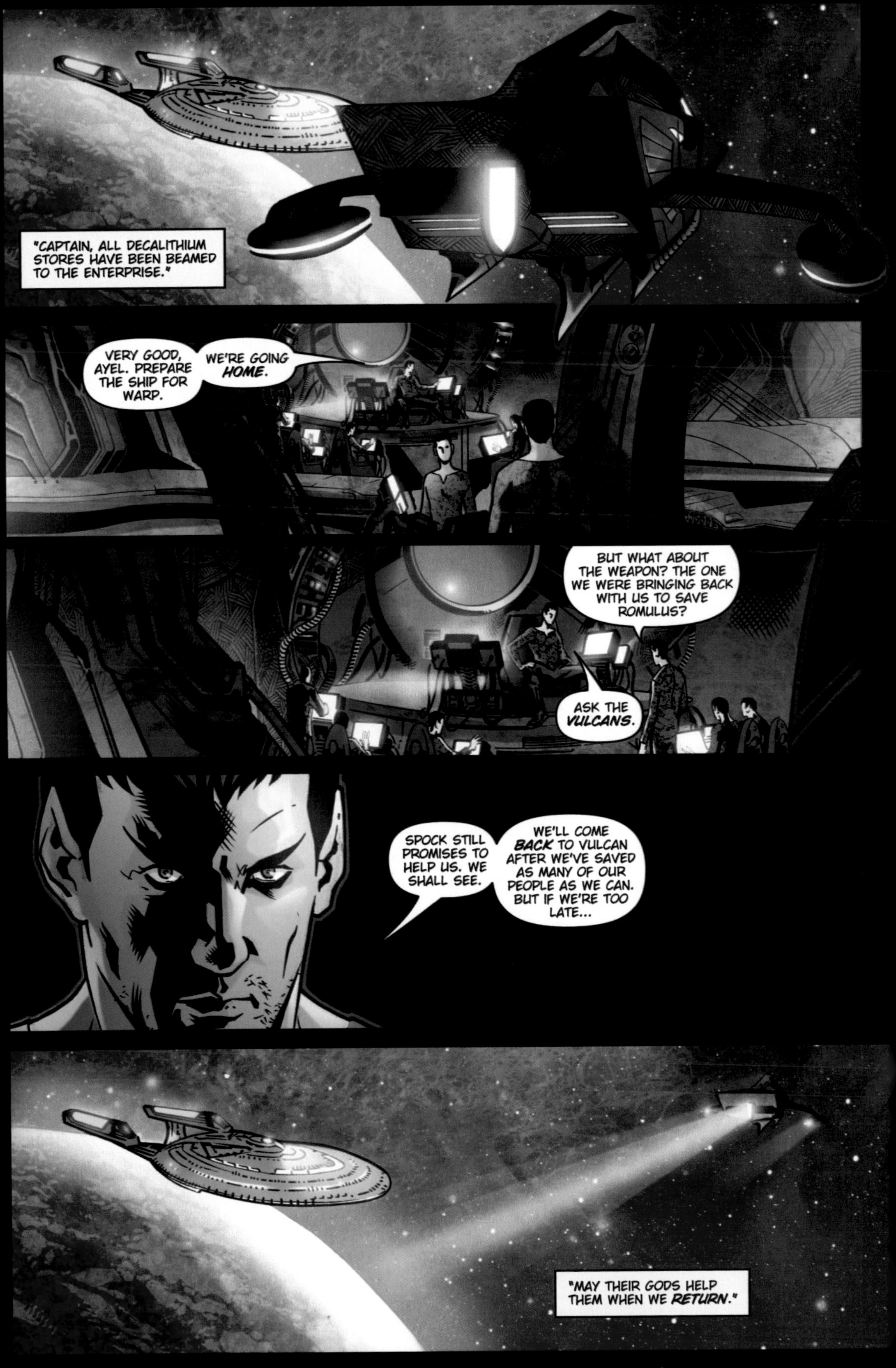
"CAPTAIN, ALL DECALITHIUM STORES HAVE BEEN BEAMED TO THE ENTERPRISE."
VERY GOOD, AYEL. PREPARE THE SHIP FOR WARP.
WE'RE GOING HOME.
BUT WHAT ABOUT THE WEAPON? THE ONE WE WERE BRINGING BACK WITH US TO SAVE ROMULUS?
ASK THE VULCANS.
SPOCK STILL PROMISES TO HELP US. WE SHALL SEE.
WE'LL COME BACK TO VULCAN AFTER WE'VE SAVED AS MANY OF OUR PEOPLE AS WE CAN. BUT IF WE'RE TOO LATE...
"MAY THEIR GODS HELP THEM WHEN WE RETURN."

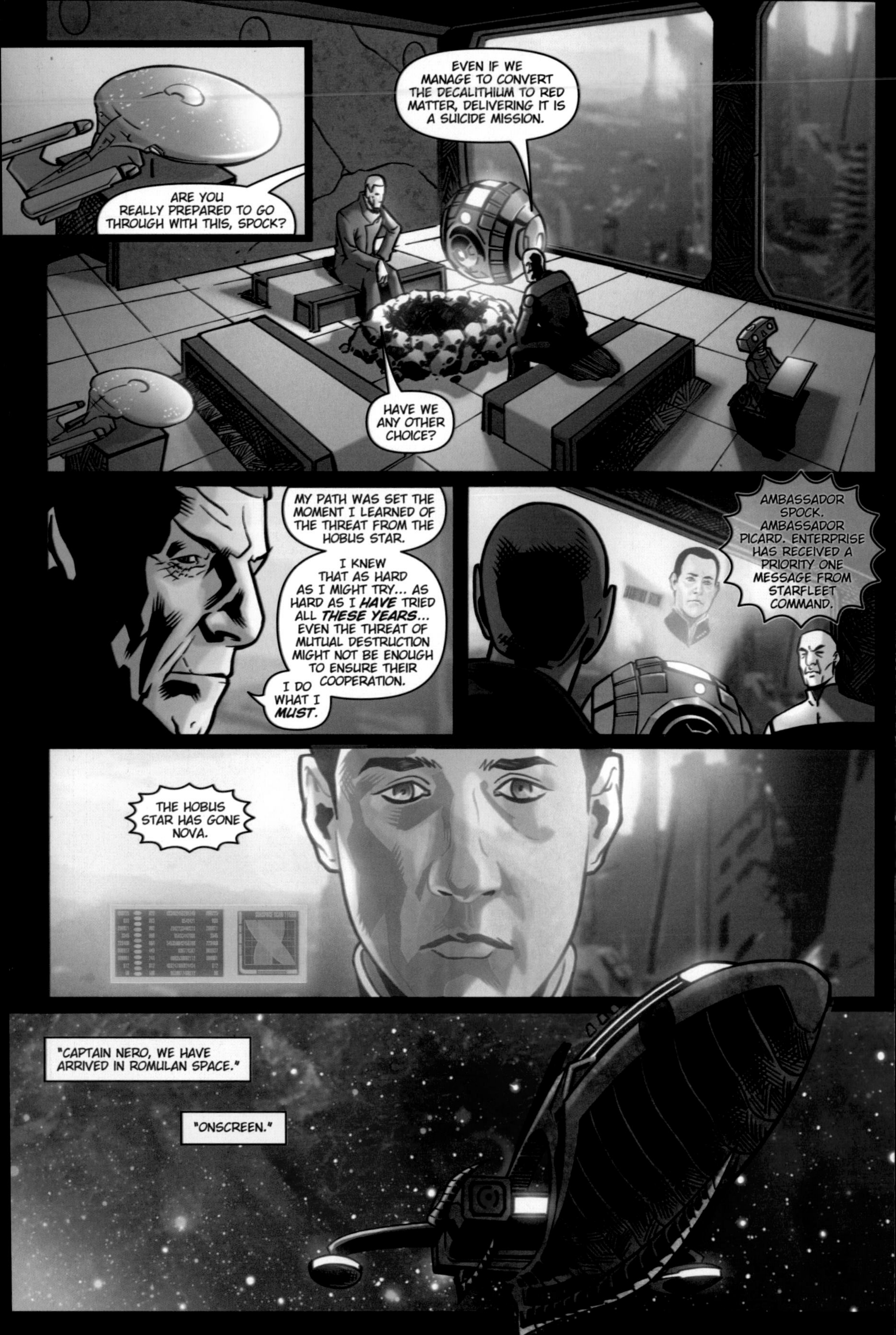
ARE YOU REALLY PREPARED TO GO THROUGH WITH THIS, SPOCK?
EVEN IF WE MANAGE TO CONVERT THE DECALITHIUM TO RED MATTER, DELIVERING IT IS A SUICIDE MISSION.
HAVE WE ANY OTHER CHOICE?
MY PATH WAS SET THE MOMENT I LEARNED OF THE THREAT FROM THE HOBUS STAR.
I KNEW THAT AS HARD AS I MIGHT TRY... AS HARD AS I **HAVE** TRIED ALL ***THESE YEARS***... EVEN THE THREAT OF MUTUAL DESTRUCTION MIGHT NOT BE ENOUGH TO ENSURE THEIR COOPERATION.
I DO WHAT I ***MUST***.
AMBASSADOR SPOCK. AMBASSADOR PICARD. ENTERPRISE HAS RECEIVED A PRIORITY ONE MESSAGE FROM STARFLEET COMMAND.
THE HOBUS STAR HAS GONE NOVA.
"CAPTAIN NERO, WE HAVE ARRIVED IN ROMULAN SPACE."
"ONSCREEN."

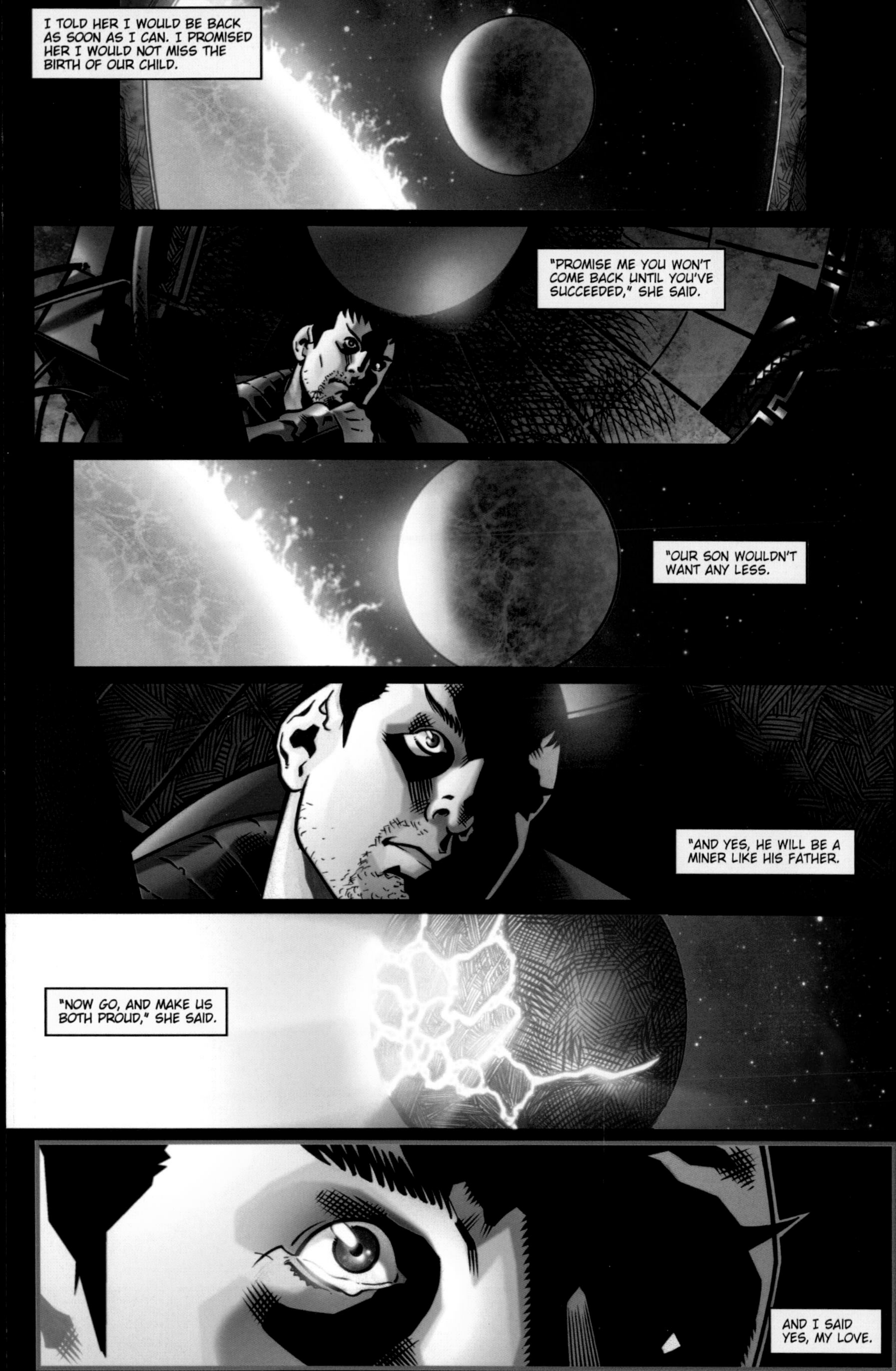
I TOLD HER I WOULD BE BACK AS SOON AS I CAN. I PROMISED HER I WOULD NOT MISS THE BIRTH OF OUR CHILD.
"PROMISE ME YOU WON'T COME BACK UNTIL YOU'VE SUCCEEDED," SHE SAID.
"OUR SON WOULDN'T WANT ANY LESS.
"AND YES, HE WILL BE A MINER LIKE HIS FATHER.
"NOW GO, AND MAKE US BOTH PROUD," SHE SAID.
AND I SAID YES, MY LOVE.

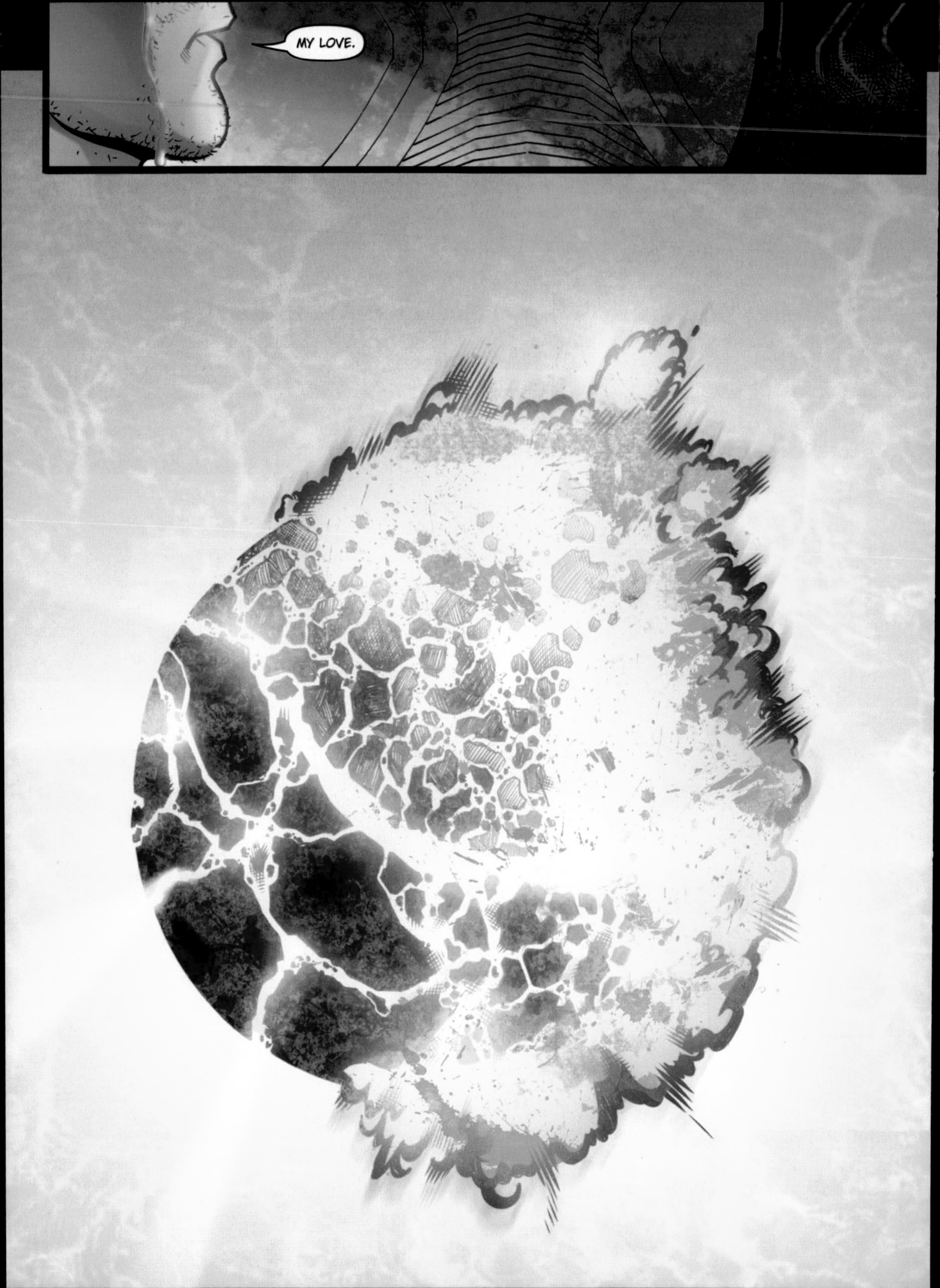
MY LOVE.

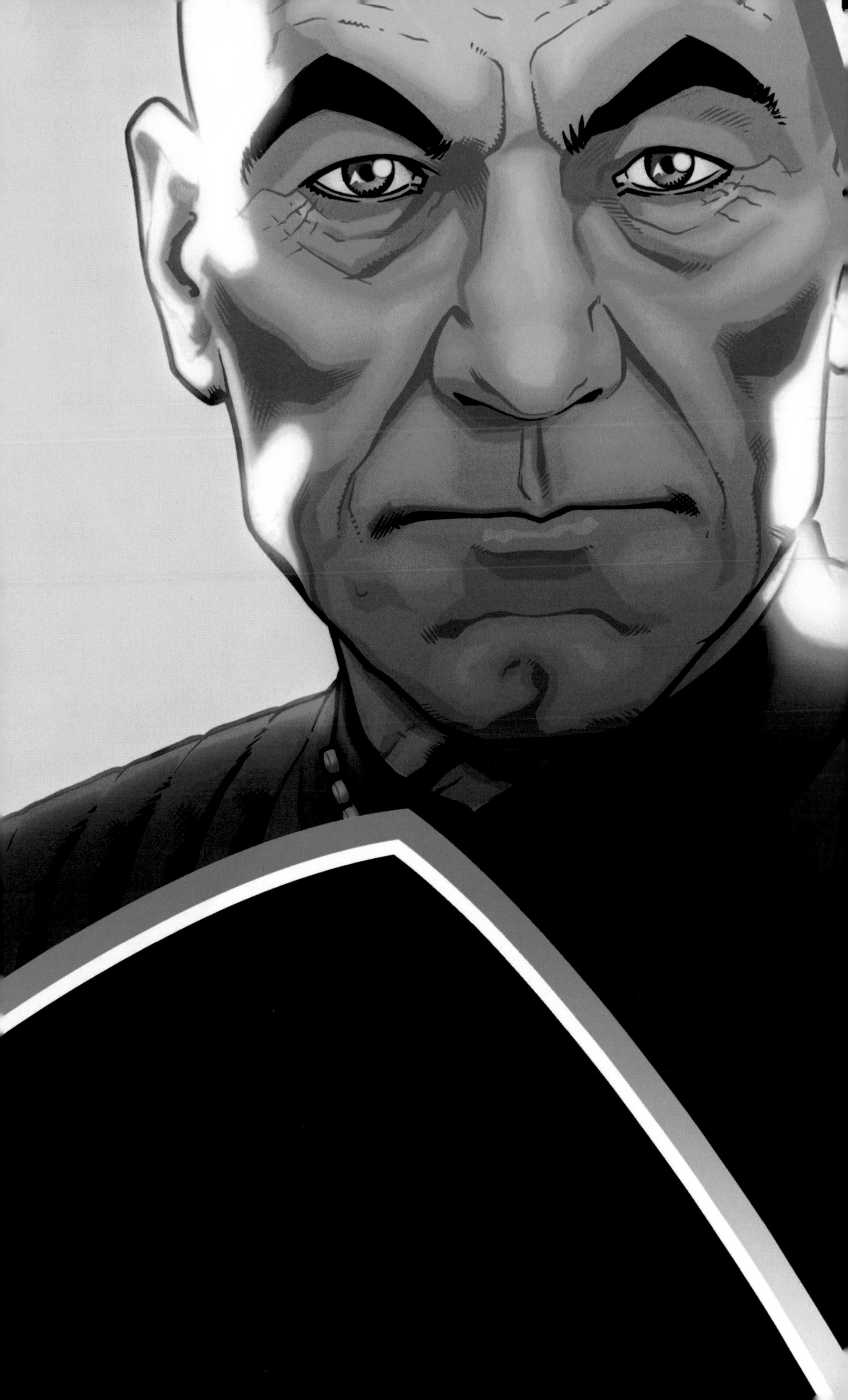

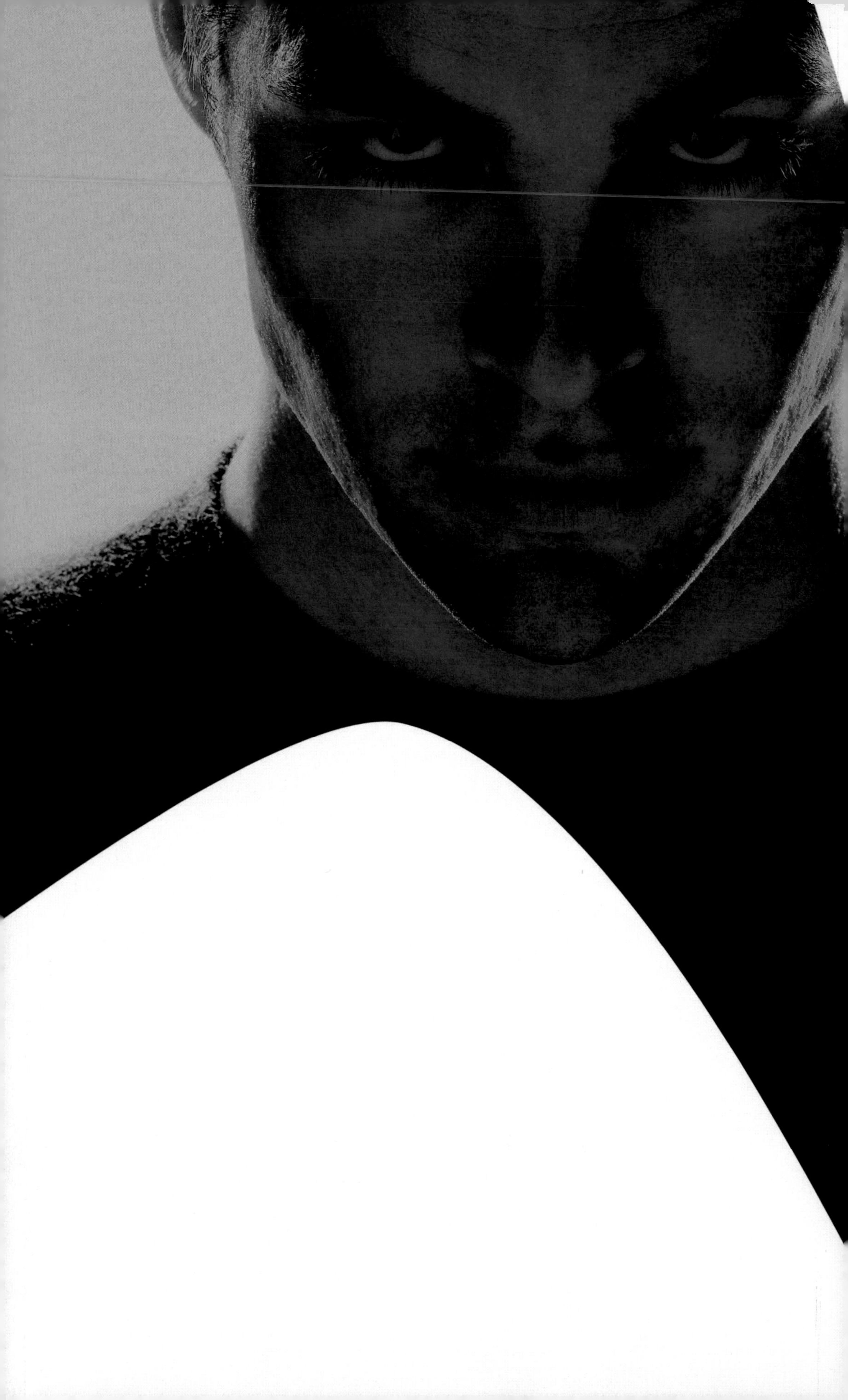

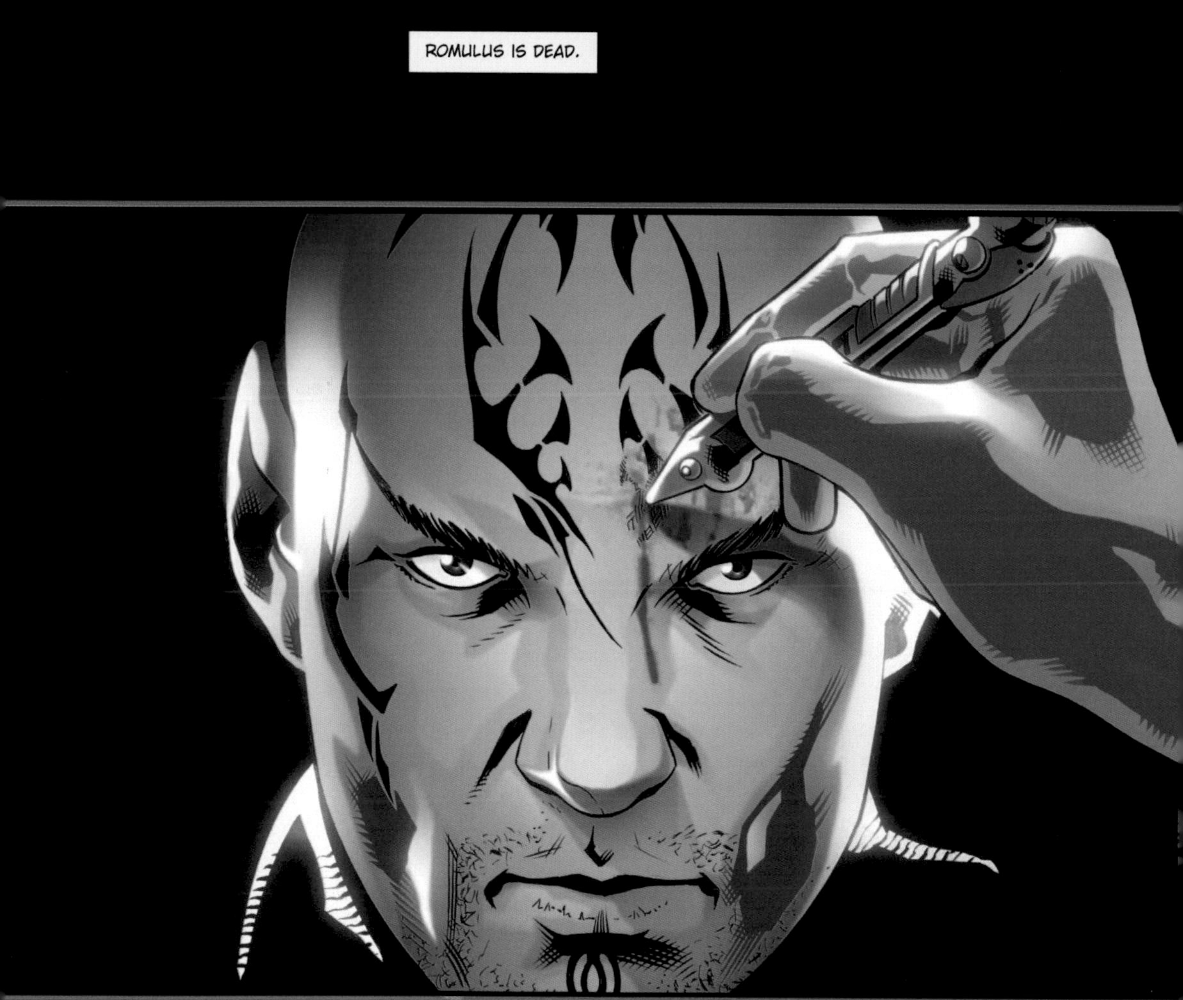
ROMULUS IS DEAD.

STAR TREK
COUNTDOWN
NUMBER THREE

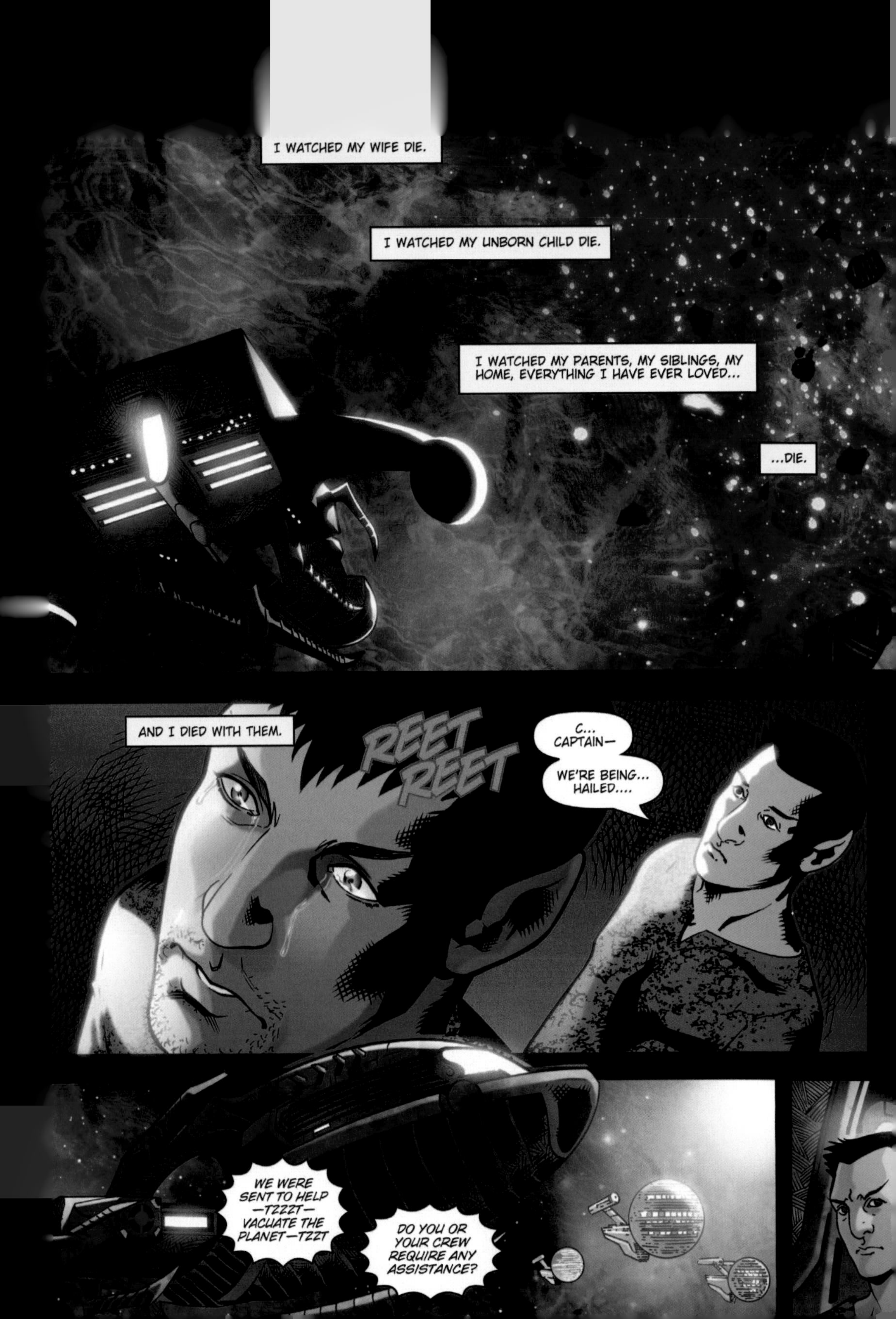

I WATCHED MY WIFE DIE.
I WATCHED MY UNBORN CHILD DIE.
I WATCHED MY PARENTS, MY SIBLINGS, MY HOME, EVERYTHING I HAVE EVER LOVED...
...DIE.
AND I DIED WITH THEM.
REET REET
C... CAPTAIN—
WE'RE BEING... HAILED....
WE WERE SENT TO HELP —TZZZT— VACUATE THE PLANET—TZZT
DO YOU OR YOUR CREW REQUIRE ANY ASSISTANCE?

TZZZT—LLO? CAN YOU HEAR US? THIS IS CAPTAIN NEWTON OF THE—TZZT—FEDERATION MEDICAL FRIGATE GALEN. DO YOU NEED HELP?

AT THAT MOMENT, THE TEARS STOPPED. I FELT SUDDENLY, STRANGELY...

...CALM.

WHAT ARE FEDERATION SHIPS DOING IN ROMULAN SPACE?

I HAVE SEVERAL INJURED REFUGEES IN NEED OF MEDICAL ATTENTION. CAN I BEAM THEM TO YOUR SHIPS NOW?

AS A MATTER OF FACT... YES.

OF COURSE. I'M SENDING YOU COORDINATES TO OUR MEDICAL BAYS NOW.

INJURED REFUGEES? WHY DID YOU TELL HIM THAT?

SO THEY WOULD LOWER THEIR SHIELDS.

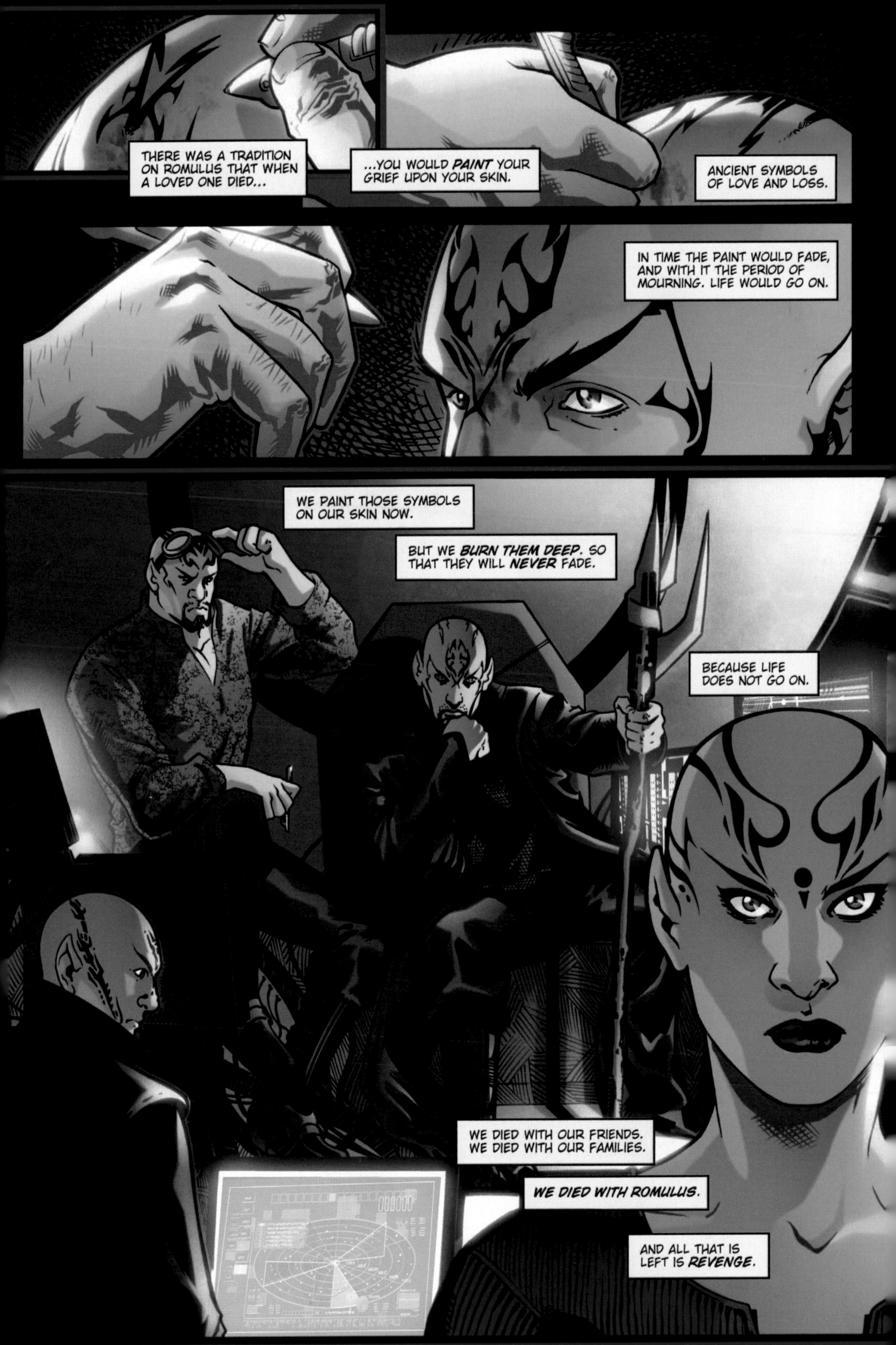

THERE WAS A TRADITION ON ROMULUS THAT WHEN A LOVED ONE DIED...
...YOU WOULD *PAINT* YOUR GRIEF UPON YOUR SKIN.
ANCIENT SYMBOLS OF LOVE AND LOSS.
IN TIME THE PAINT WOULD FADE, AND WITH IT THE PERIOD OF MOURNING. LIFE WOULD GO ON.
WE PAINT THOSE SYMBOLS ON OUR SKIN NOW.
BUT WE *BURN THEM DEEP*. SO THAT THEY WILL *NEVER* FADE.
BECAUSE LIFE DOES NOT GO ON.
WE DIED WITH OUR FRIENDS. WE DIED WITH OUR FAMILIES.
WE DIED WITH ROMULUS.
AND ALL THAT IS LEFT IS *REVENGE*.

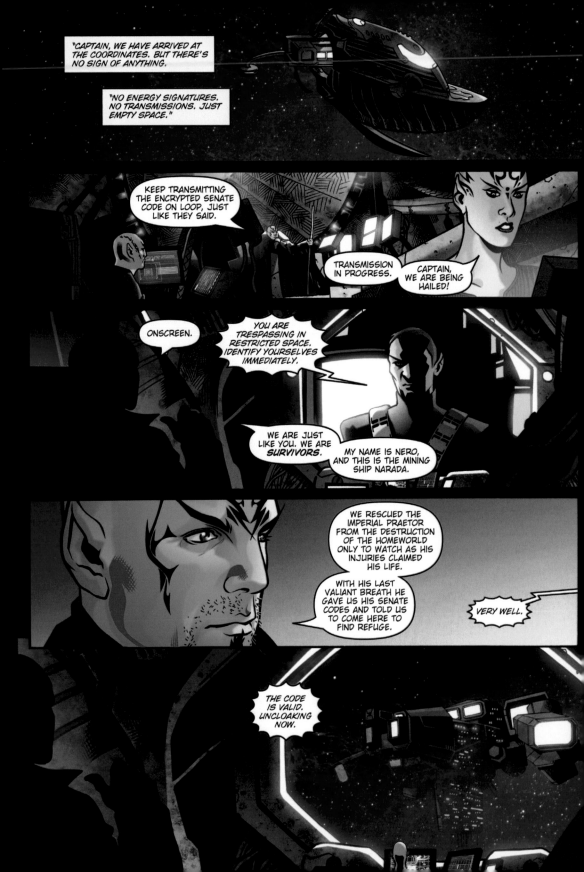

"CAPTAIN, WE HAVE ARRIVED AT THE COORDINATES. BUT THERE'S NO SIGN OF ANYTHING.

"NO ENERGY SIGNATURES. NO TRANSMISSIONS. JUST EMPTY SPACE."

KEEP TRANSMITTING THE ENCRYPTED SENATE CODE ON LOOP, JUST LIKE THEY SAID.

TRANSMISSION IN PROGRESS.

CAPTAIN, WE ARE BEING HAILED!

ONSCREEN.

YOU ARE TRESPASSING IN RESTRICTED SPACE. IDENTIFY YOURSELVES IMMEDIATELY.

WE ARE JUST LIKE YOU. WE ARE SURVIVORS.

MY NAME IS NERO, AND THIS IS THE MINING SHIP NARADA.

WE RESCUED THE IMPERIAL PRAETOR FROM THE DESTRUCTION OF THE HOMEWORLD ONLY TO WATCH AS HIS INJURIES CLAIMED HIS LIFE.

WITH HIS LAST VALIANT BREATH HE GAVE US HIS SENATE CODES AND TOLD US TO COME HERE TO FIND REFUGE.

VERY WELL.

THE CODE IS VALID. UNCLOAKING NOW.

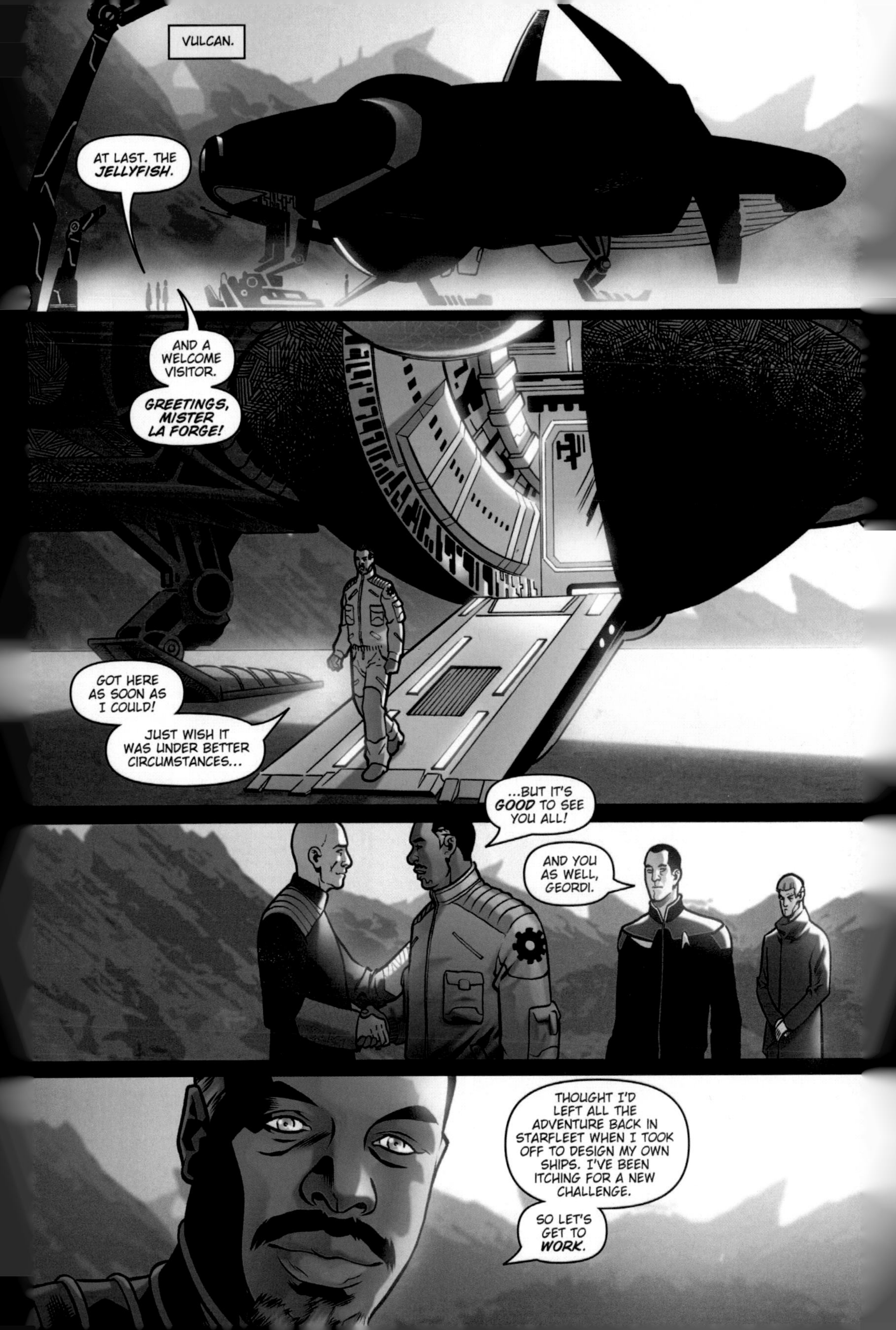
VULCAN.
AT LAST. THE JELLYFISH.
AND A WELCOME VISITOR.
GREETINGS, MISTER LA FORGE!
GOT HERE AS SOON AS I COULD!
JUST WISH IT WAS UNDER BETTER CIRCUMSTANCES...
...BUT IT'S GOOD TO SEE YOU ALL!
AND YOU AS WELL, GEORDI.
THOUGHT I'D LEFT ALL THE ADVENTURE BACK IN STARFLEET WHEN I TOOK OFF TO DESIGN MY OWN SHIPS. I'VE BEEN ITCHING FOR A NEW CHALLENGE.
SO LET'S GET TO WORK.

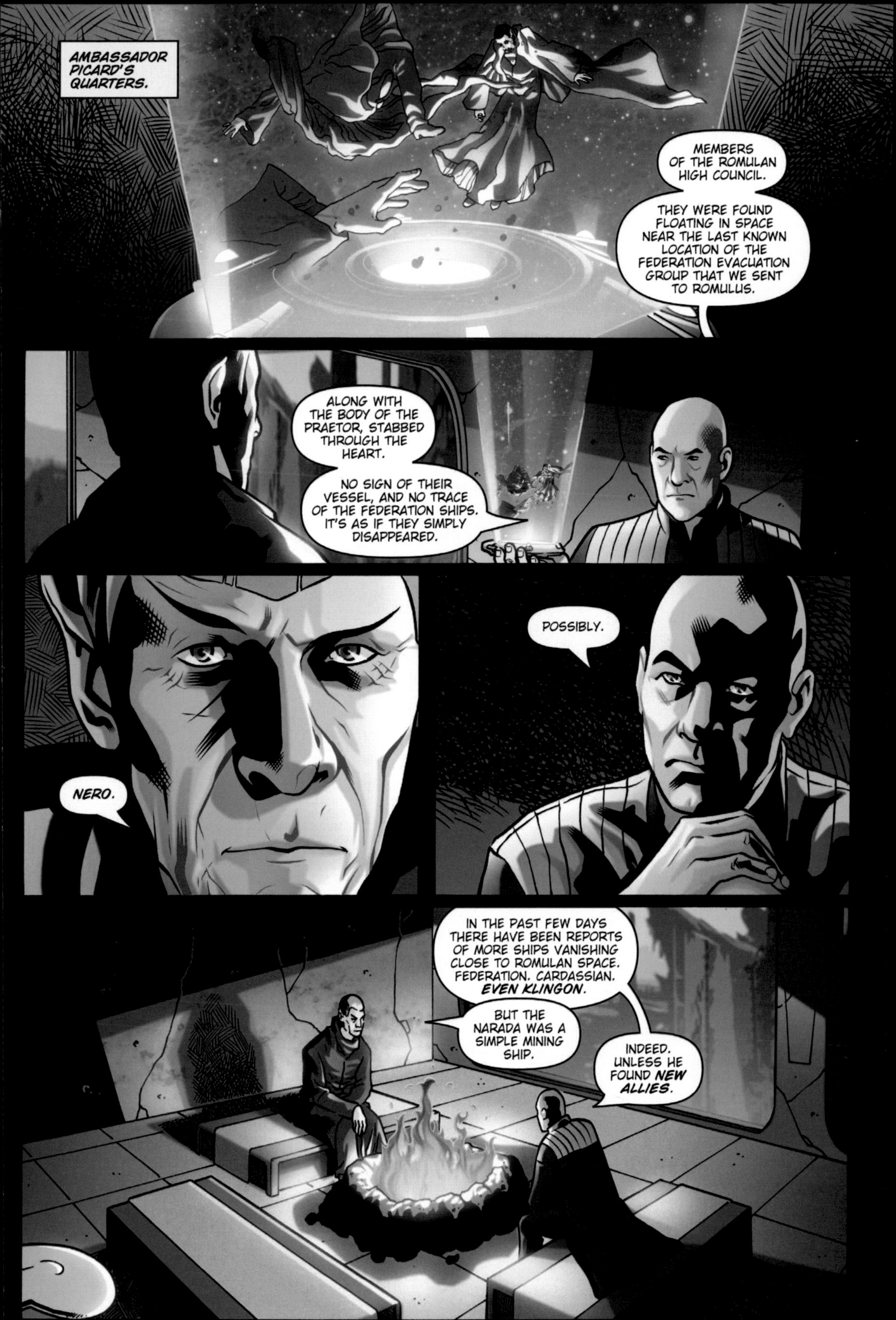
AMBASSADOR PICARD'S QUARTERS.
MEMBERS OF THE ROMULAN HIGH COUNCIL.
THEY WERE FOUND FLOATING IN SPACE NEAR THE LAST KNOWN LOCATION OF THE FEDERATION EVACUATION GROUP THAT WE SENT TO ROMULUS.
ALONG WITH THE BODY OF THE PRAETOR, STABBED THROUGH THE HEART.
NO SIGN OF THEIR VESSEL, AND NO TRACE OF THE FEDERATION SHIPS. IT'S AS IF THEY SIMPLY DISAPPEARED.
POSSIBLY.
NERO.
IN THE PAST FEW DAYS THERE HAVE BEEN REPORTS OF MORE SHIPS VANISHING CLOSE TO ROMULAN SPACE. FEDERATION. CARDASSIAN. EVEN KLINGON.
BUT THE NARADA WAS A SIMPLE MINING SHIP.
INDEED. UNLESS HE FOUND NEW ALLIES.

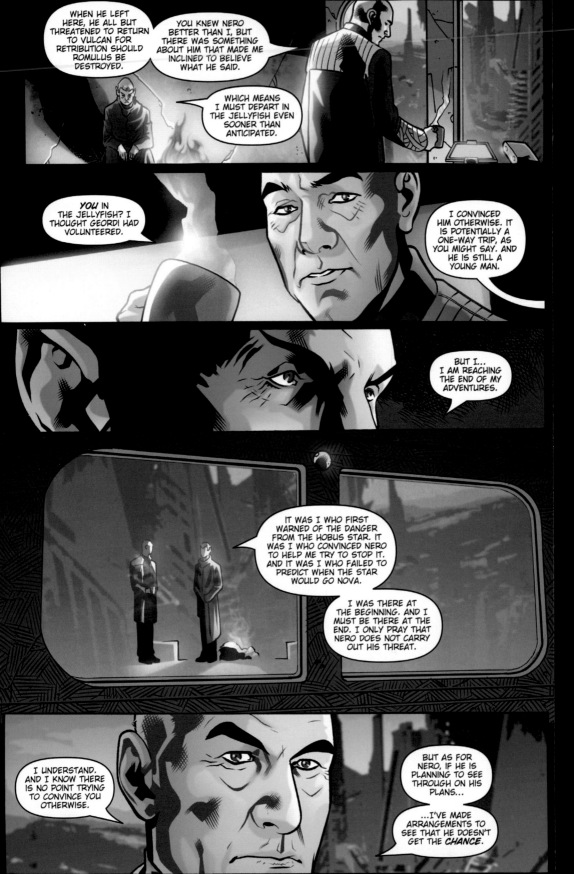

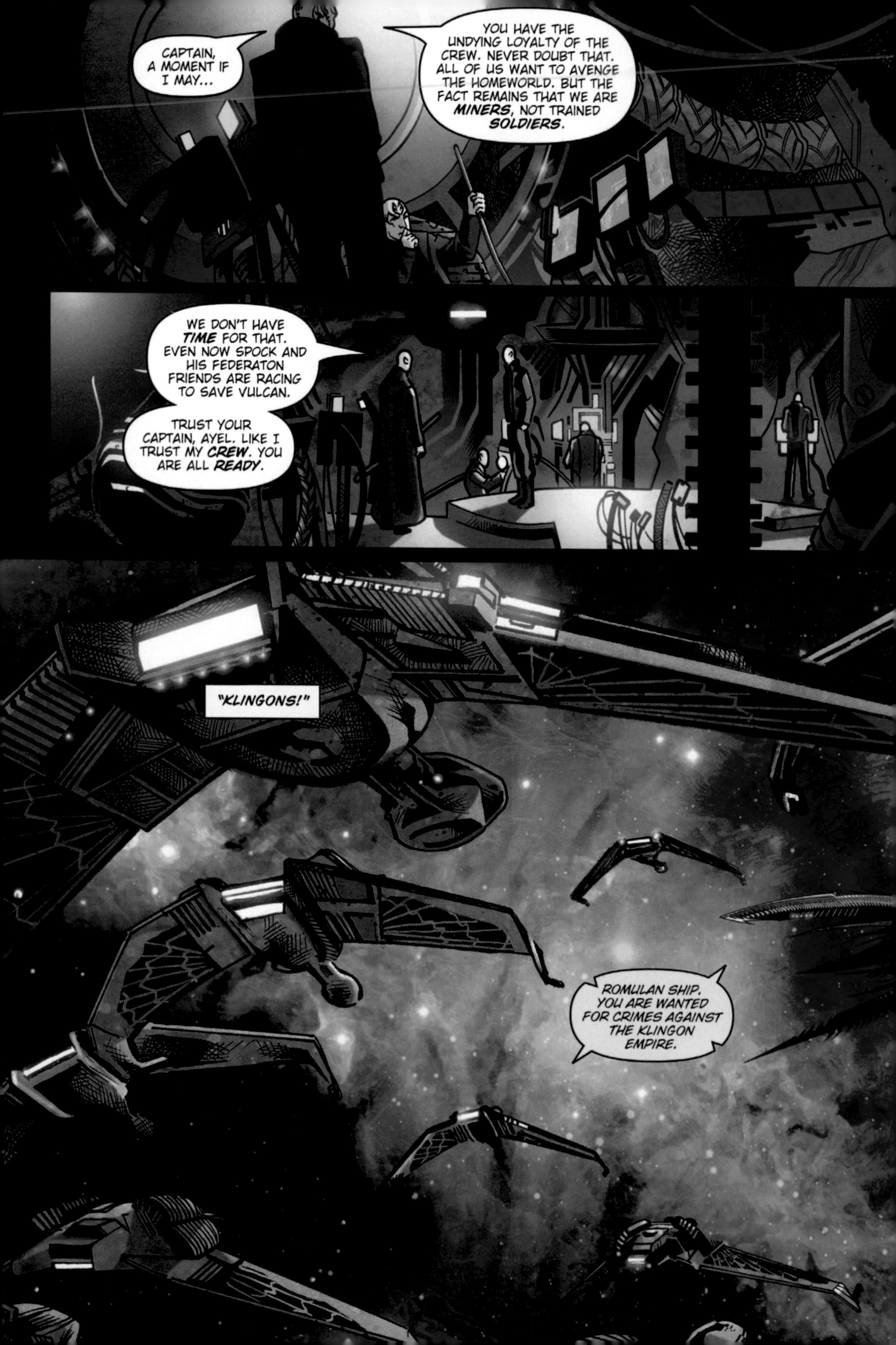
CAPTAIN, A MOMENT IF I MAY...
YOU HAVE THE UNDYING LOYALTY OF THE CREW. NEVER DOUBT THAT. ALL OF US WANT TO AVENGE THE HOMEWORLD. BUT THE FACT REMAINS THAT WE ARE *MINERS*, NOT TRAINED *SOLDIERS*.
WE DON'T HAVE *TIME* FOR THAT. EVEN NOW SPOCK AND HIS FEDERATON FRIENDS ARE RACING TO SAVE VULCAN.
TRUST YOUR CAPTAIN, AYEL. LIKE I TRUST MY *CREW*. YOU ARE ALL *READY*.
"KLINGONS!"
ROMULAN SHIP. YOU ARE WANTED FOR CRIMES AGAINST THE KLINGON EMPIRE.

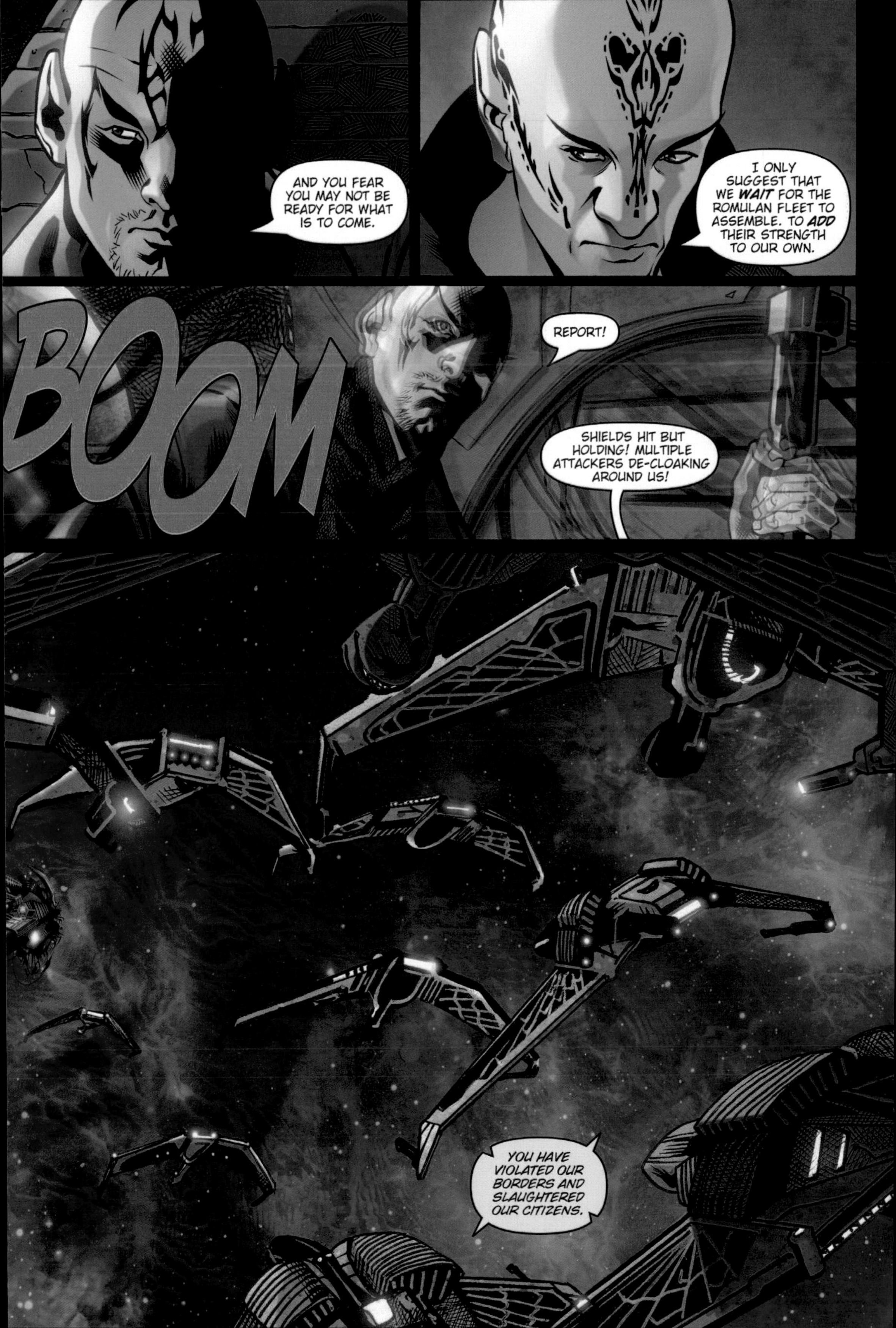
AND YOU FEAR YOU MAY NOT BE READY FOR WHAT IS TO COME.
I ONLY SUGGEST THAT WE WAIT FOR THE ROMULAN FLEET TO ASSEMBLE. TO ADD THEIR STRENGTH TO OUR OWN.
BOOM
REPORT!
SHIELDS HIT BUT HOLDING! MULTIPLE ATTACKERS DE-CLOAKING AROUND US!
YOU HAVE VIOLATED OUR BORDERS AND SLAUGHTERED OUR CITIZENS.

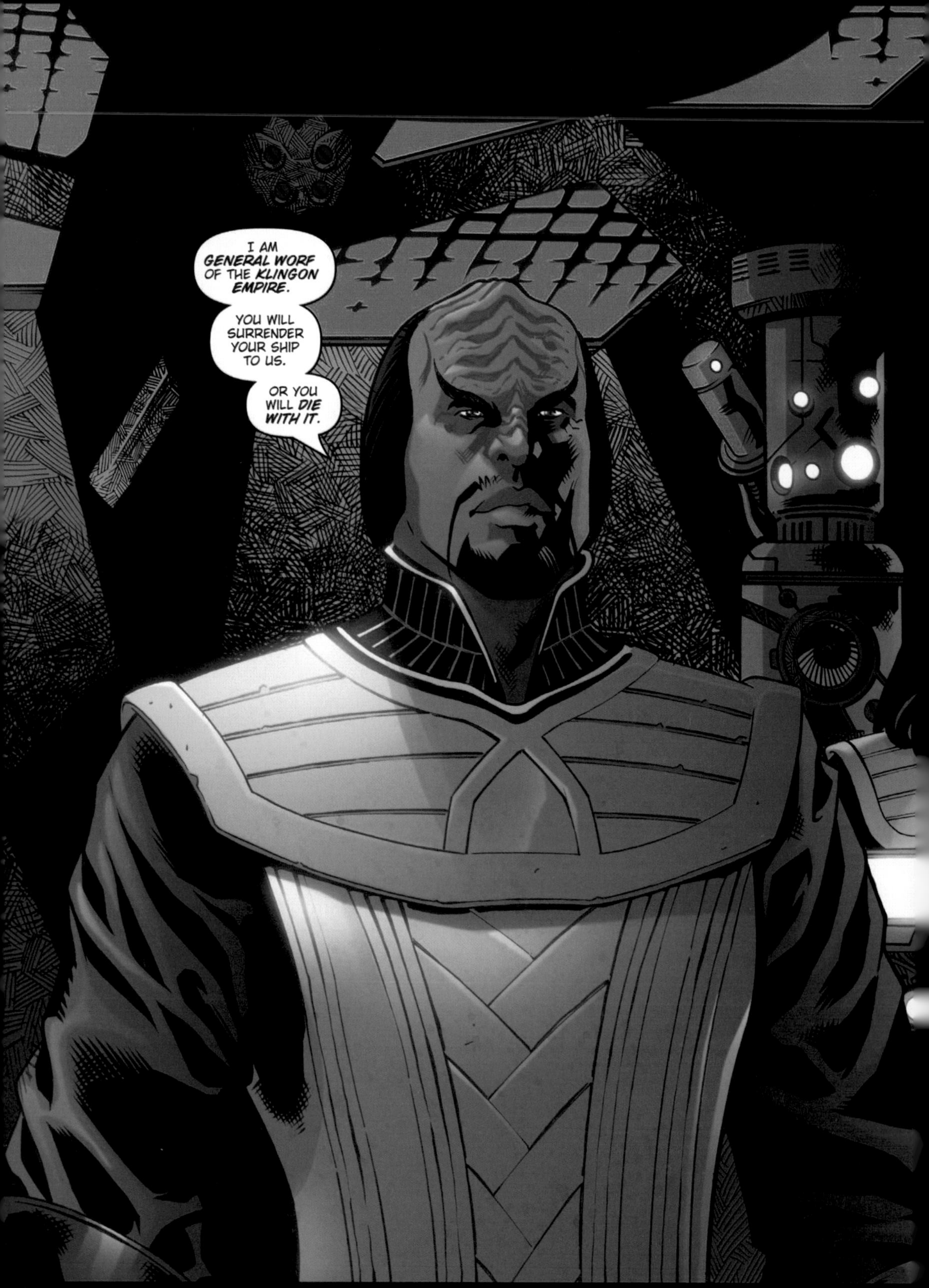
I AM GENERAL WORF OF THE KLINGON EMPIRE.
YOU WILL SURRENDER YOUR SHIP TO US.
OR YOU WILL DIE WITH IT.

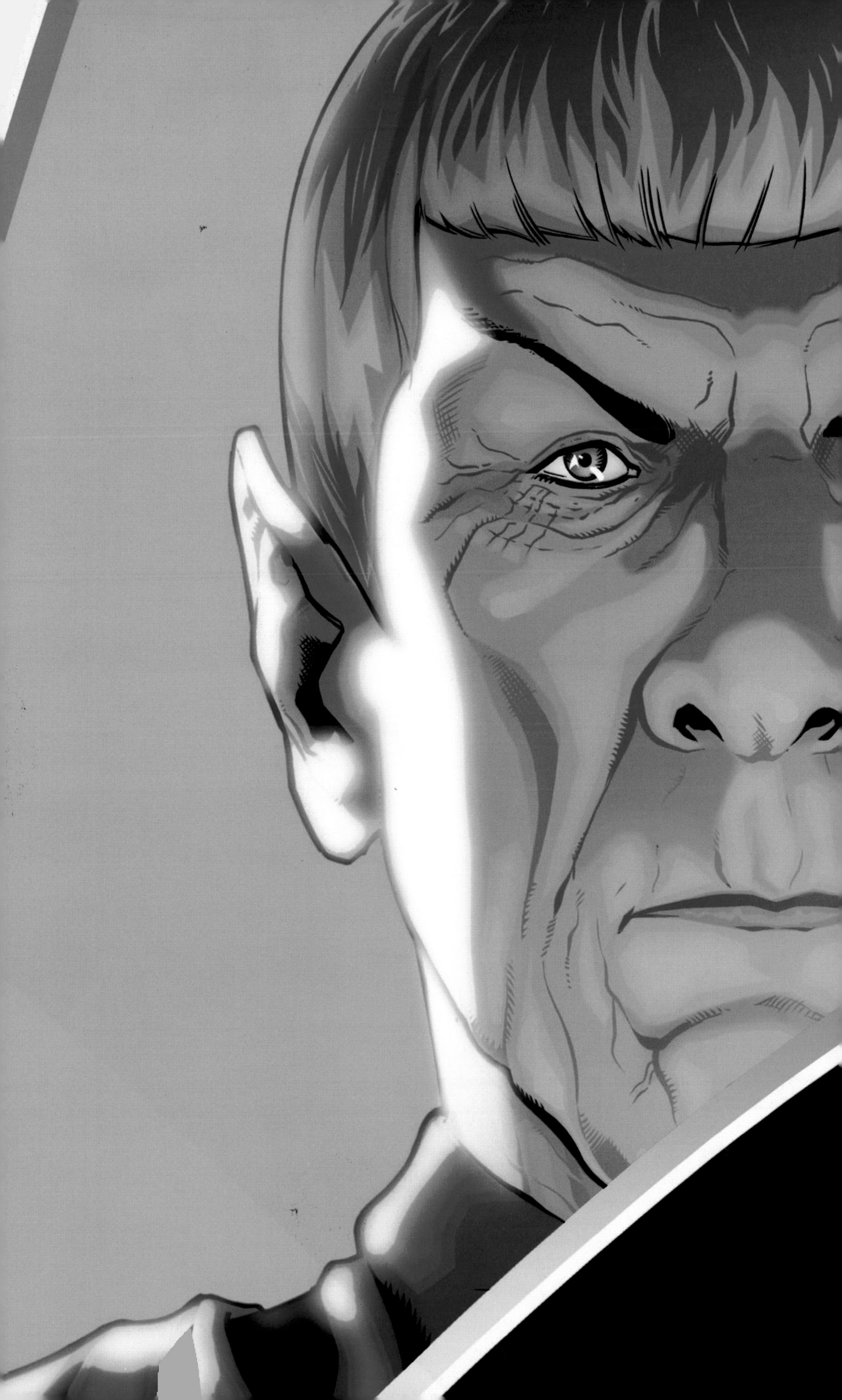

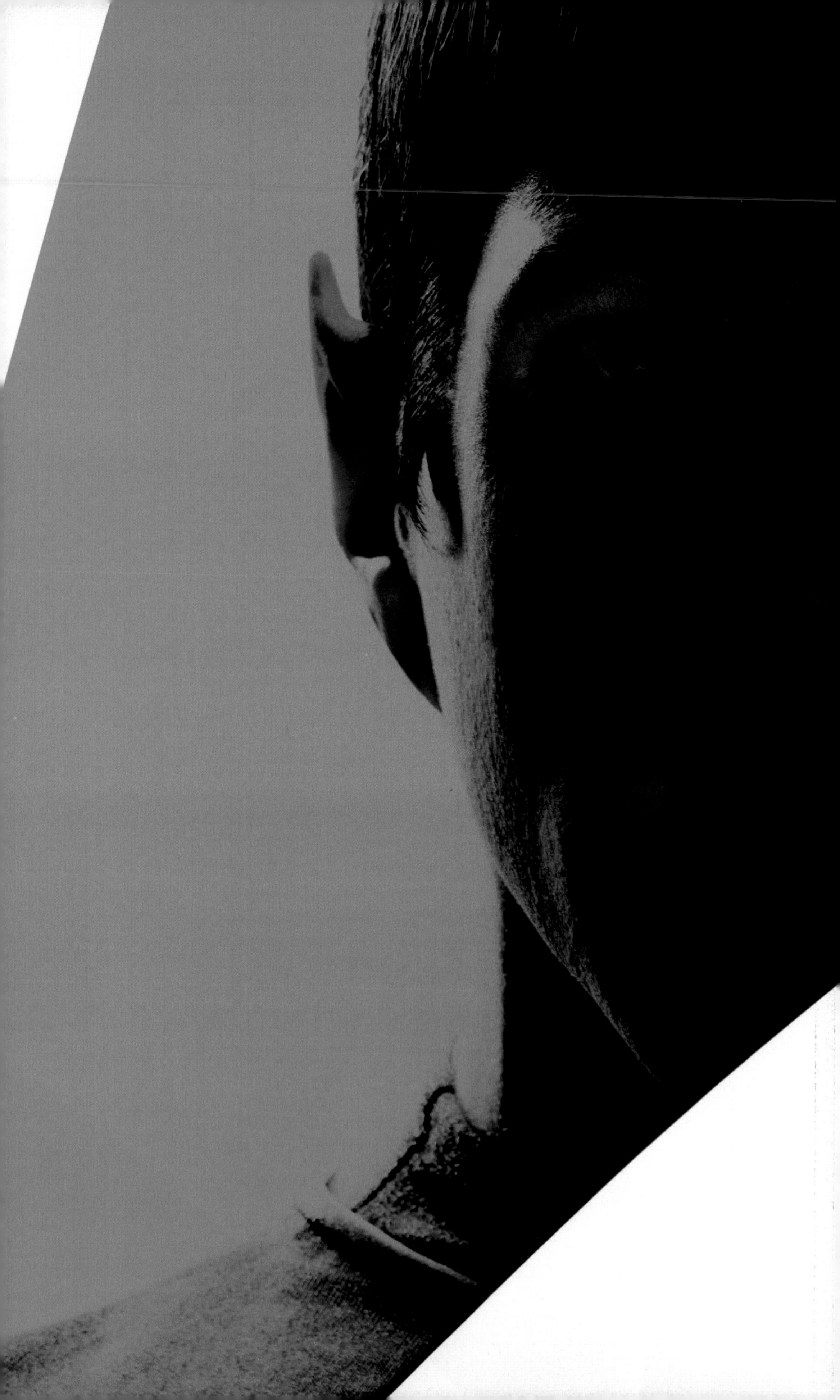

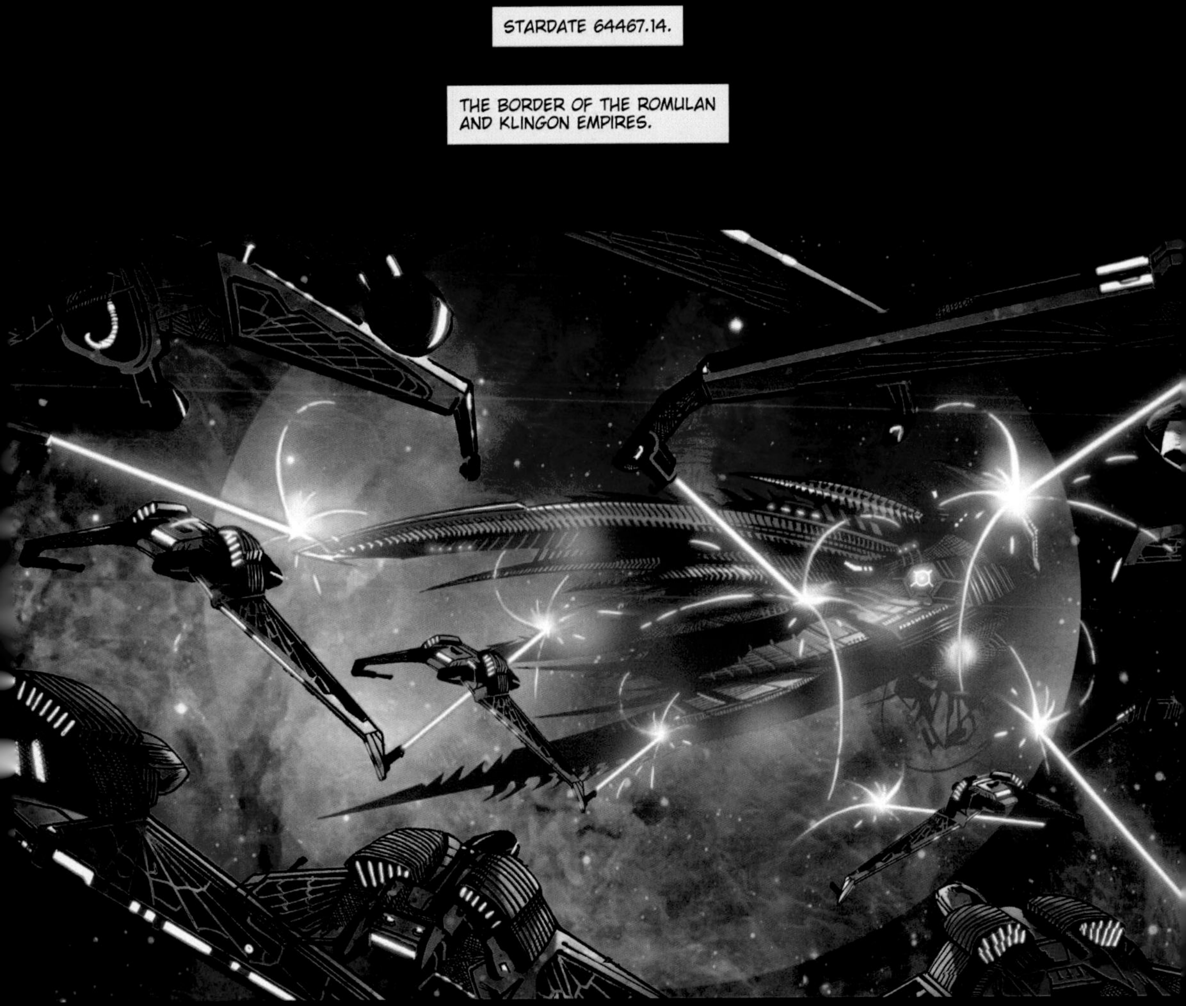
STARDATE 64467.14.
THE BORDER OF THE ROMULAN AND KLINGON EMPIRES.

STAR TREK
COUNTDOWN
NUMBER FOUR

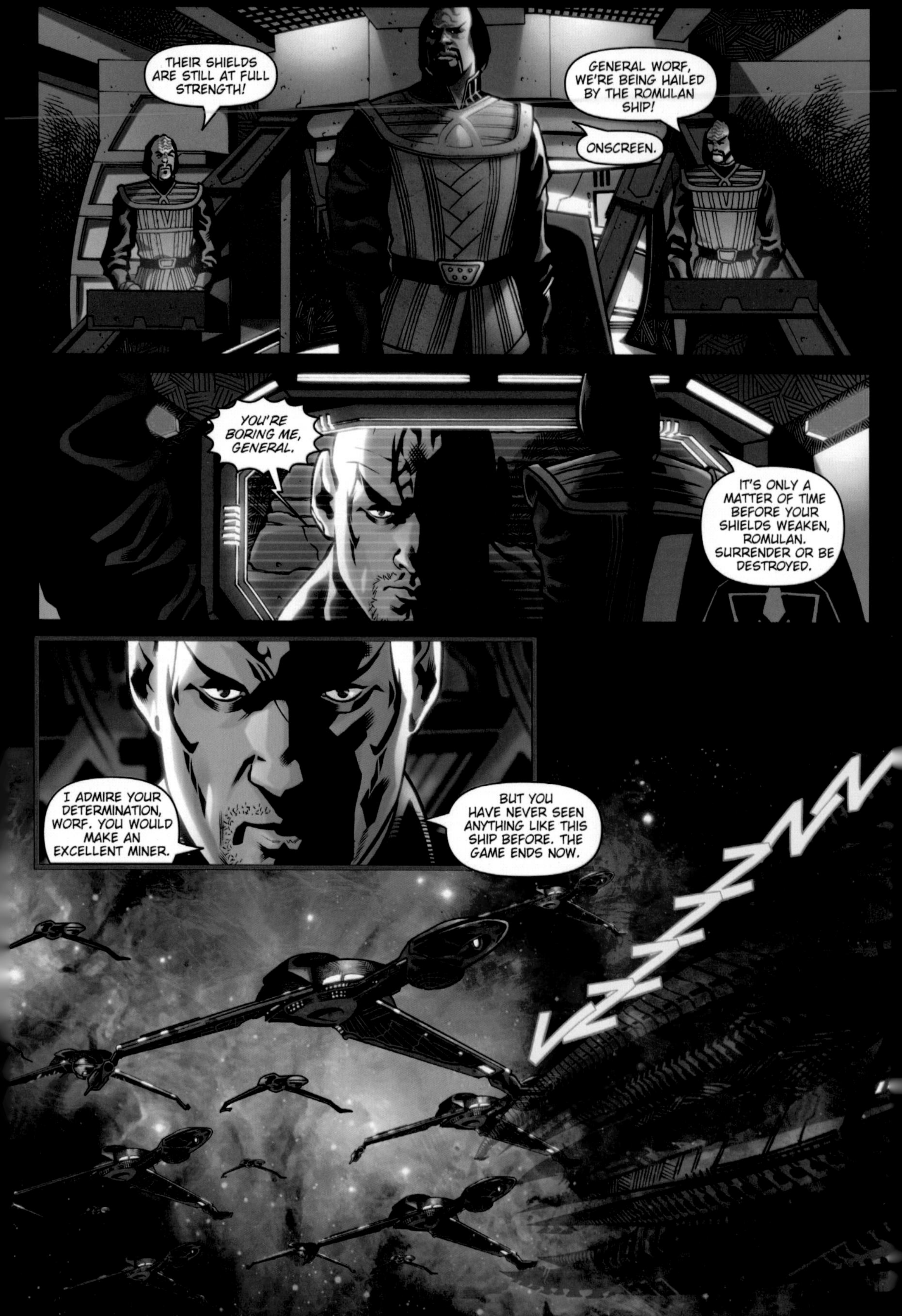

THEIR SHIELDS ARE STILL AT FULL STRENGTH!
GENERAL WORF, WE'RE BEING HAILED BY THE ROMULAN SHIP!
ONSCREEN.
YOU'RE BORING ME, GENERAL.
IT'S ONLY A MATTER OF TIME BEFORE YOUR SHIELDS WEAKEN, ROMULAN. SURRENDER OR BE DESTROYED.
I ADMIRE YOUR DETERMINATION, WORF. YOU WOULD MAKE AN EXCELLENT MINER.
BUT YOU HAVE NEVER SEEN ANYTHING LIKE THIS SHIP BEFORE. THE GAME ENDS NOW.

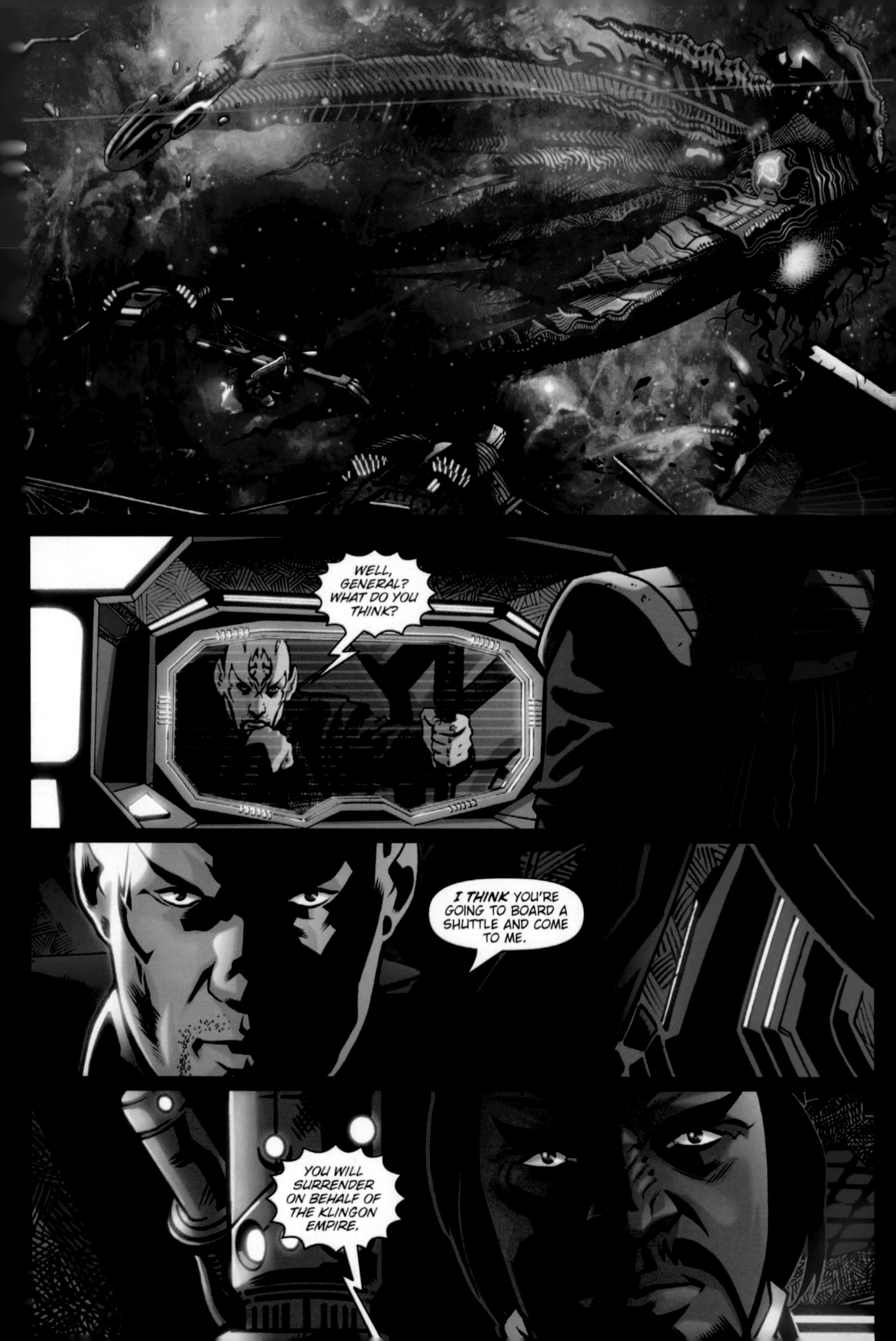
WELL, GENERAL? WHAT DO YOU THINK?
I THINK YOU'RE GOING TO BOARD A SHUTTLE AND COME TO ME.
YOU WILL SURRENDER ON BEHALF OF THE KLINGON EMPIRE.

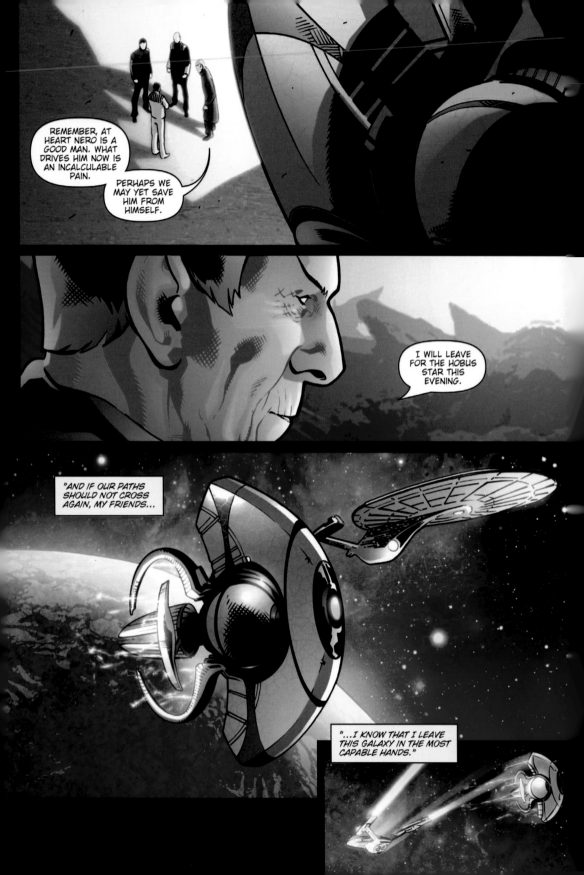

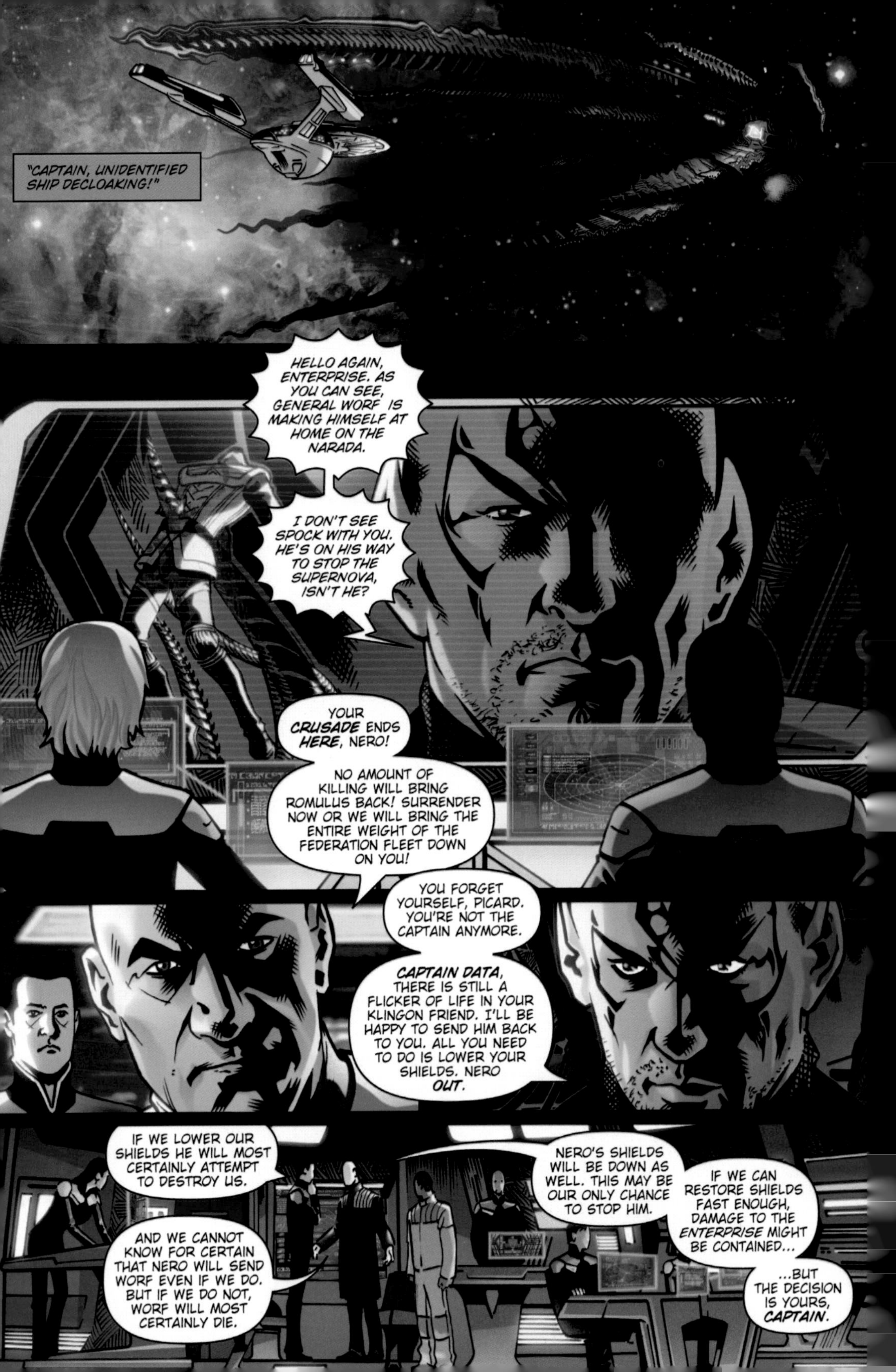
"CAPTAIN, UNIDENTIFIED SHIP DECLOAKING!"
HELLO AGAIN, ENTERPRISE. AS YOU CAN SEE, GENERAL WORF IS MAKING HIMSELF AT HOME ON THE NARADA.
I DON'T SEE SPOCK WITH YOU. HE'S ON HIS WAY TO STOP THE SUPERNOVA, ISN'T HE?
YOUR **CRUSADE** ENDS **HERE**, NERO!
NO AMOUNT OF KILLING WILL BRING ROMULUS BACK! SURRENDER NOW OR WE WILL BRING THE ENTIRE WEIGHT OF THE FEDERATION FLEET DOWN ON YOU!
YOU FORGET YOURSELF, PICARD. YOU'RE NOT THE CAPTAIN ANYMORE.
CAPTAIN DATA, THERE IS STILL A FLICKER OF LIFE IN YOUR KLINGON FRIEND. I'LL BE HAPPY TO SEND HIM BACK TO YOU. ALL YOU NEED TO DO IS LOWER YOUR SHIELDS. NERO **OUT**.
IF WE LOWER OUR SHIELDS HE WILL MOST CERTAINLY ATTEMPT TO DESTROY US.
AND WE CANNOT KNOW FOR CERTAIN THAT NERO WILL SEND WORF EVEN IF WE DO. BUT IF WE DO NOT, WORF WILL MOST CERTAINLY DIE.
NERO'S SHIELDS WILL BE DOWN AS WELL. THIS MAY BE OUR ONLY CHANCE TO STOP HIM.
IF WE CAN RESTORE SHIELDS FAST ENOUGH, DAMAGE TO THE *ENTERPRISE* MIGHT BE CONTAINED...
...BUT THE DECISION IS YOURS, ***CAPTAIN***.

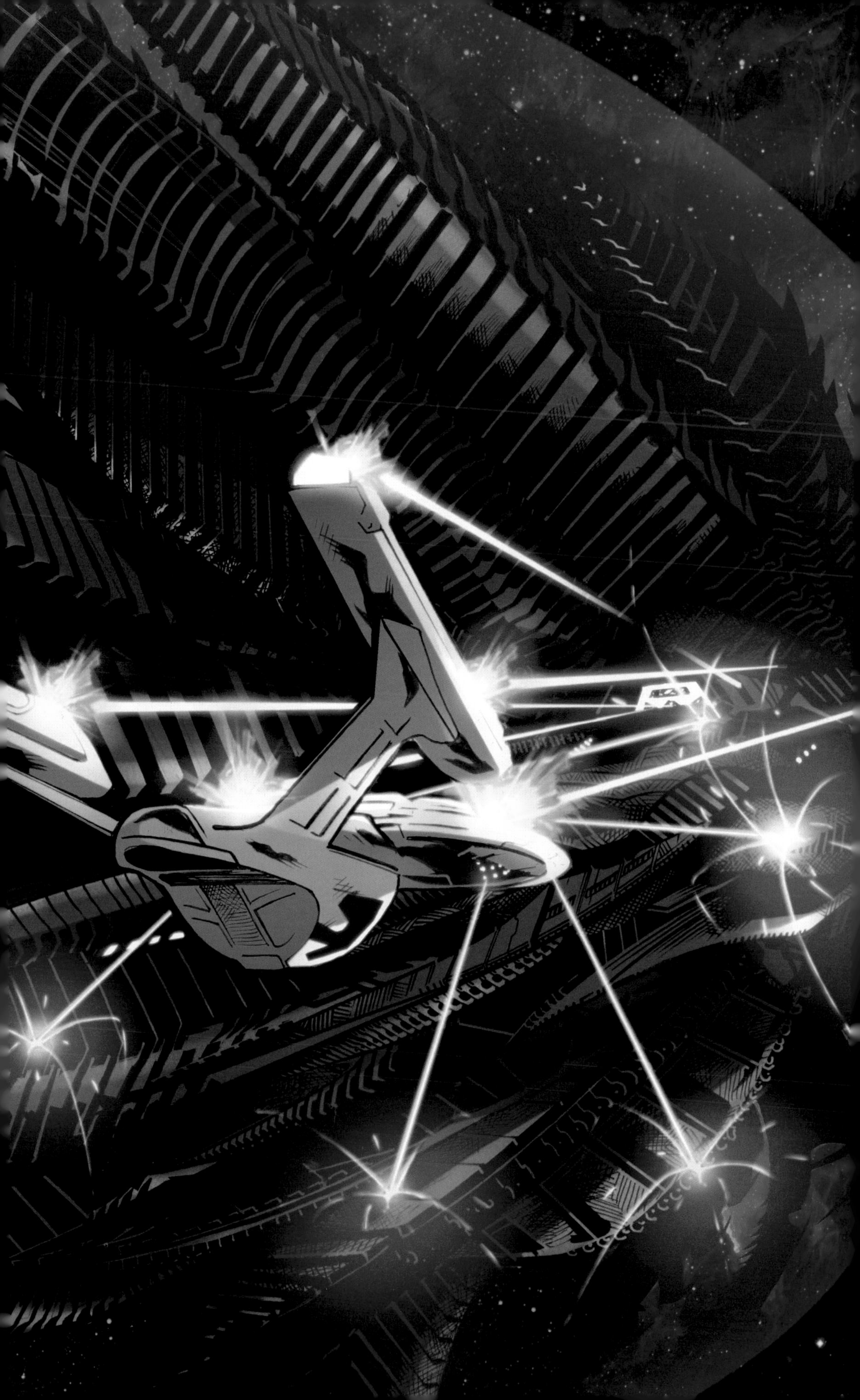

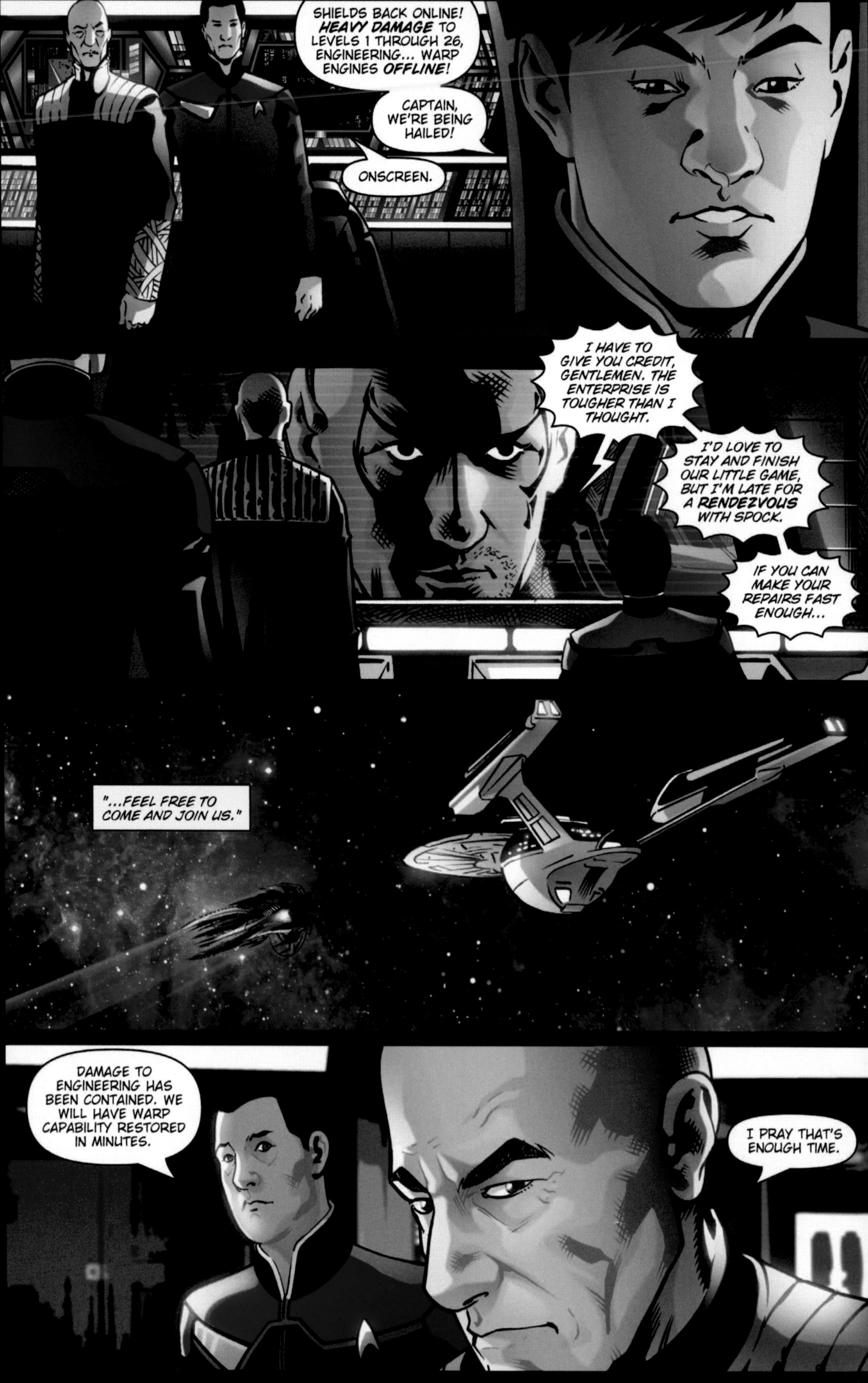
SHIELDS BACK ONLINE! HEAVY DAMAGE TO LEVELS 1 THROUGH 26, ENGINEERING... WARP ENGINES OFFLINE!
CAPTAIN, WE'RE BEING HAILED!
ONSCREEN.
I HAVE TO GIVE YOU CREDIT, GENTLEMEN. THE ENTERPRISE IS TOUGHER THAN I THOUGHT.
I'D LOVE TO STAY AND FINISH OUR LITTLE GAME, BUT I'M LATE FOR A RENDEZVOUS WITH SPOCK.
IF YOU CAN MAKE YOUR REPAIRS FAST ENOUGH...
"...FEEL FREE TO COME AND JOIN US."
DAMAGE TO ENGINEERING HAS BEEN CONTAINED. WE WILL HAVE WARP CAPABILITY RESTORED IN MINUTES.
I PRAY THAT'S ENOUGH TIME.

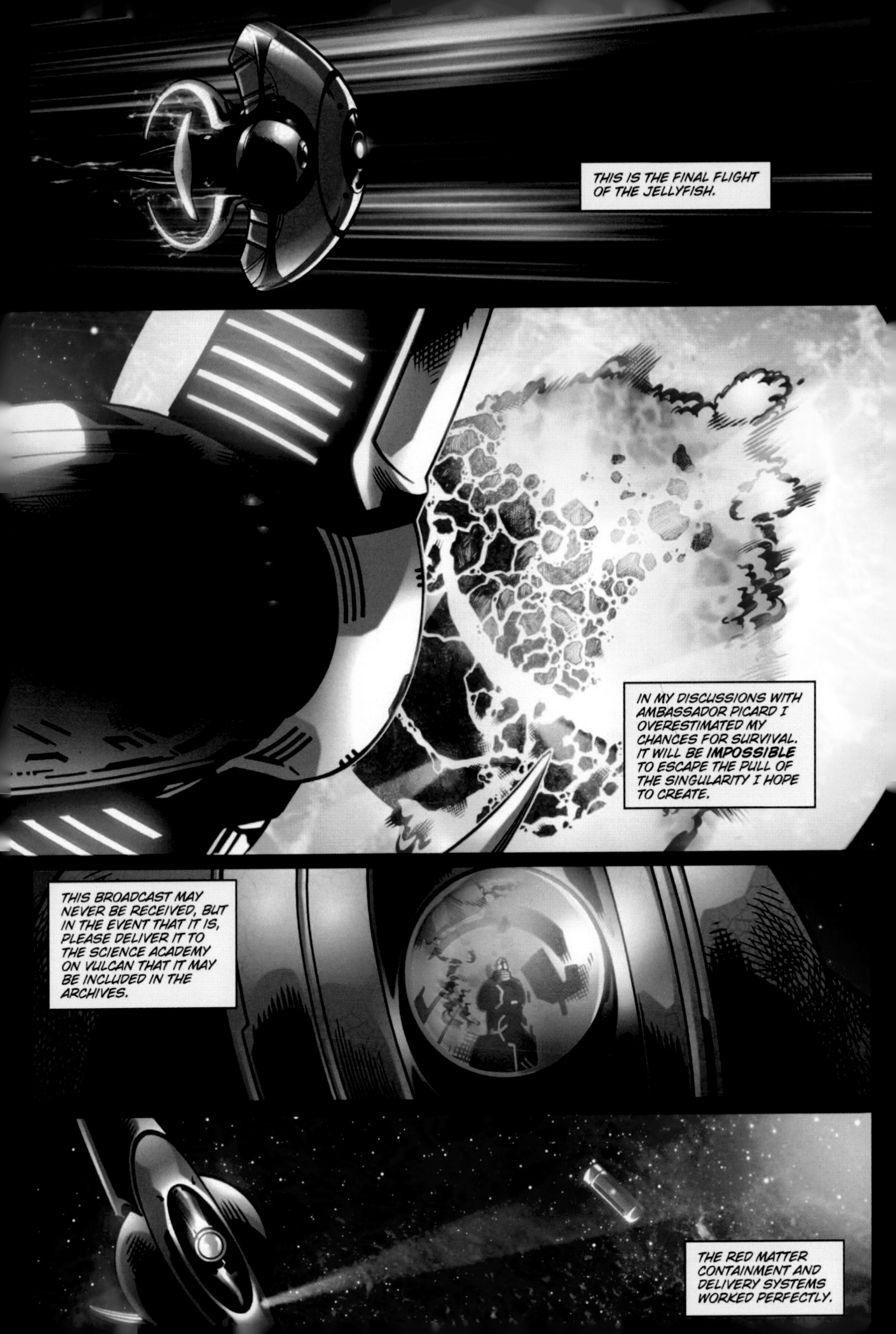
THIS IS THE FINAL FLIGHT OF THE JELLYFISH.
IN MY DISCUSSIONS WITH AMBASSADOR PICARD I OVERESTIMATED MY CHANCES FOR SURVIVAL. IT WILL BE **IMPOSSIBLE** TO ESCAPE THE PULL OF THE SINGULARITY I HOPE TO CREATE.
THIS BROADCAST MAY NEVER BE RECEIVED, BUT IN THE EVENT THAT IT IS, PLEASE DELIVER IT TO THE SCIENCE ACADEMY ON VULCAN THAT IT MAY BE INCLUDED IN THE ARCHIVES.
THE RED MATTER CONTAINMENT AND DELIVERY SYSTEMS WORKED PERFECTLY.

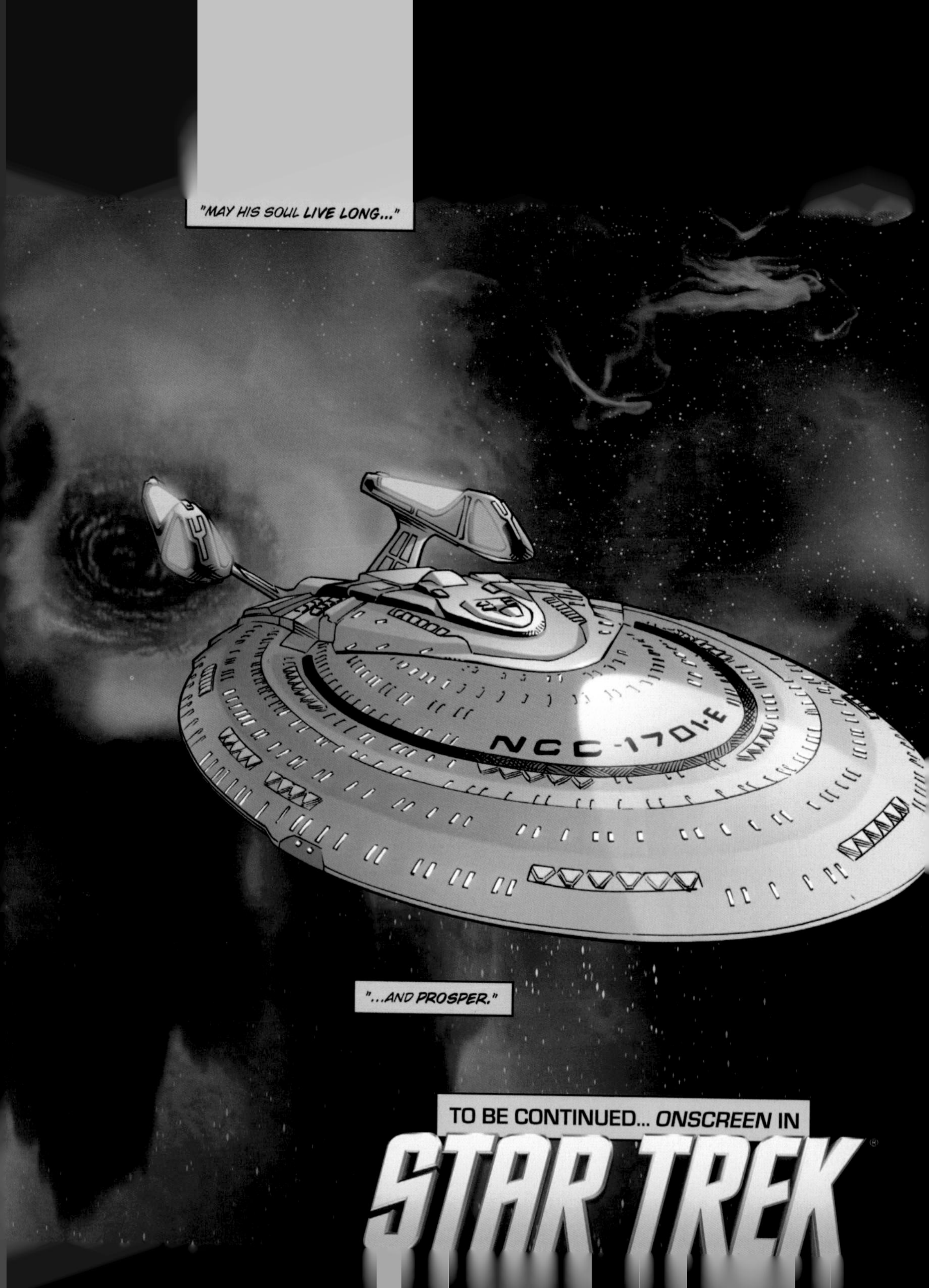
"MAY HIS SOUL LIVE LONG..."
NCC-1701-E
"...AND PROSPER."
TO BE CONTINUED... ONSCREEN IN
STAR TREK

AFTERWORD

The notion that we'd be called to serve *STAR TREK* in any form is something we never dared dream. This book has had particular meaning for us in that we fell in love with *STAR TREK* through the characters of *THE NEXT GENERATION*. The longest summer of our lives was spent waiting to find out how Captain Riker and the amazing crew of the Enterprise were going to defeat their former Captain, Jean-Luc Picard, after his transformation into Locutus of Borg.

We don't expect to ever feel the same anticipation again, but perhaps we can create some for new fans. That is the intention of this book... to take a ride with a beloved crew that no one believed could ever match the original, and to pay homage to their stewardship of a thing called *STAR TREK*. Their journey now takes us back to the beginning...

Roberto Orci & Alex Kurtzman

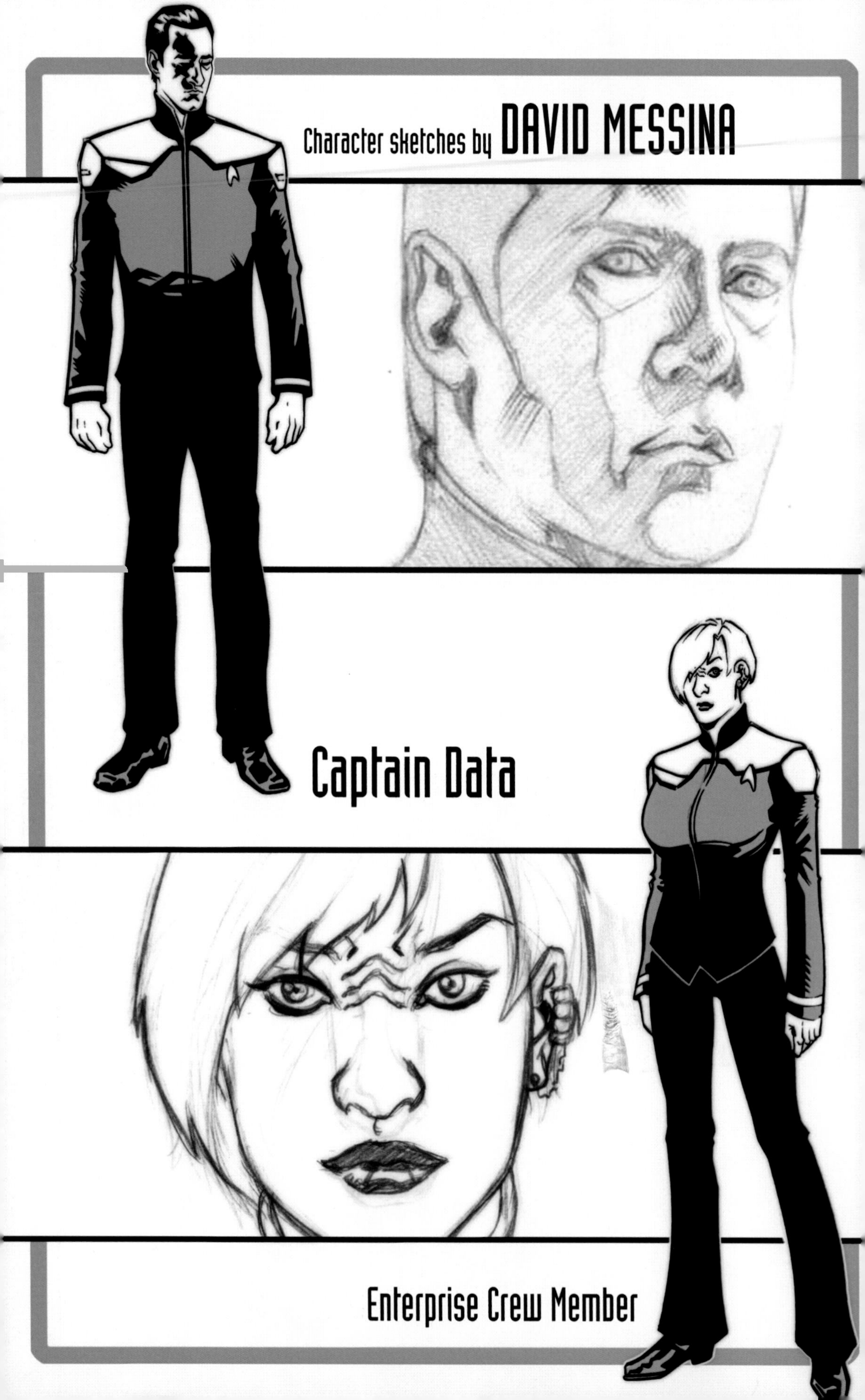
Character sketches by DAVID MESSINA
Captain Data
Enterprise Crew Member

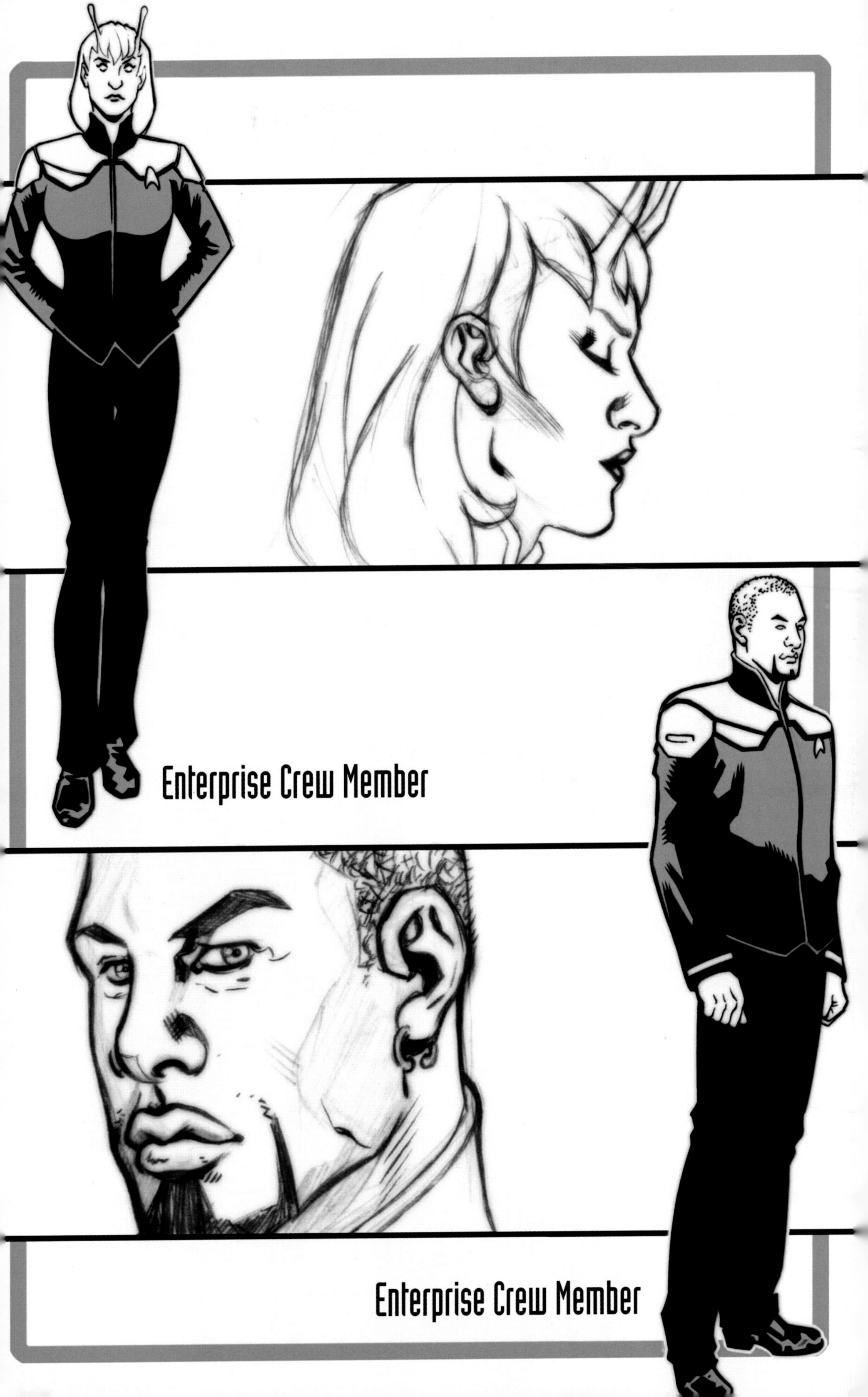
Enterprise Crew Member
Enterprise Crew Member

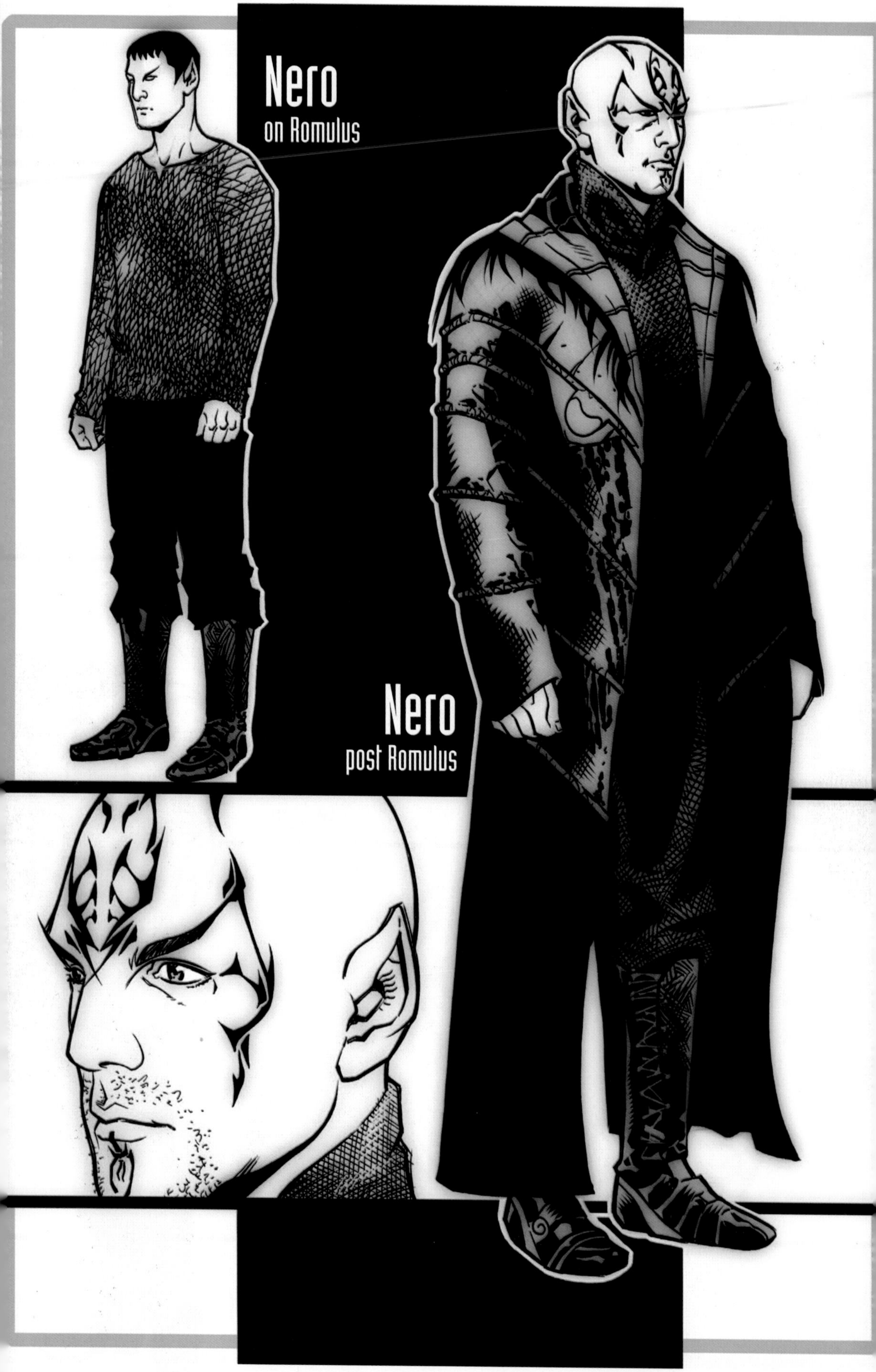

Nero
on Romulus
Nero
post Romulus

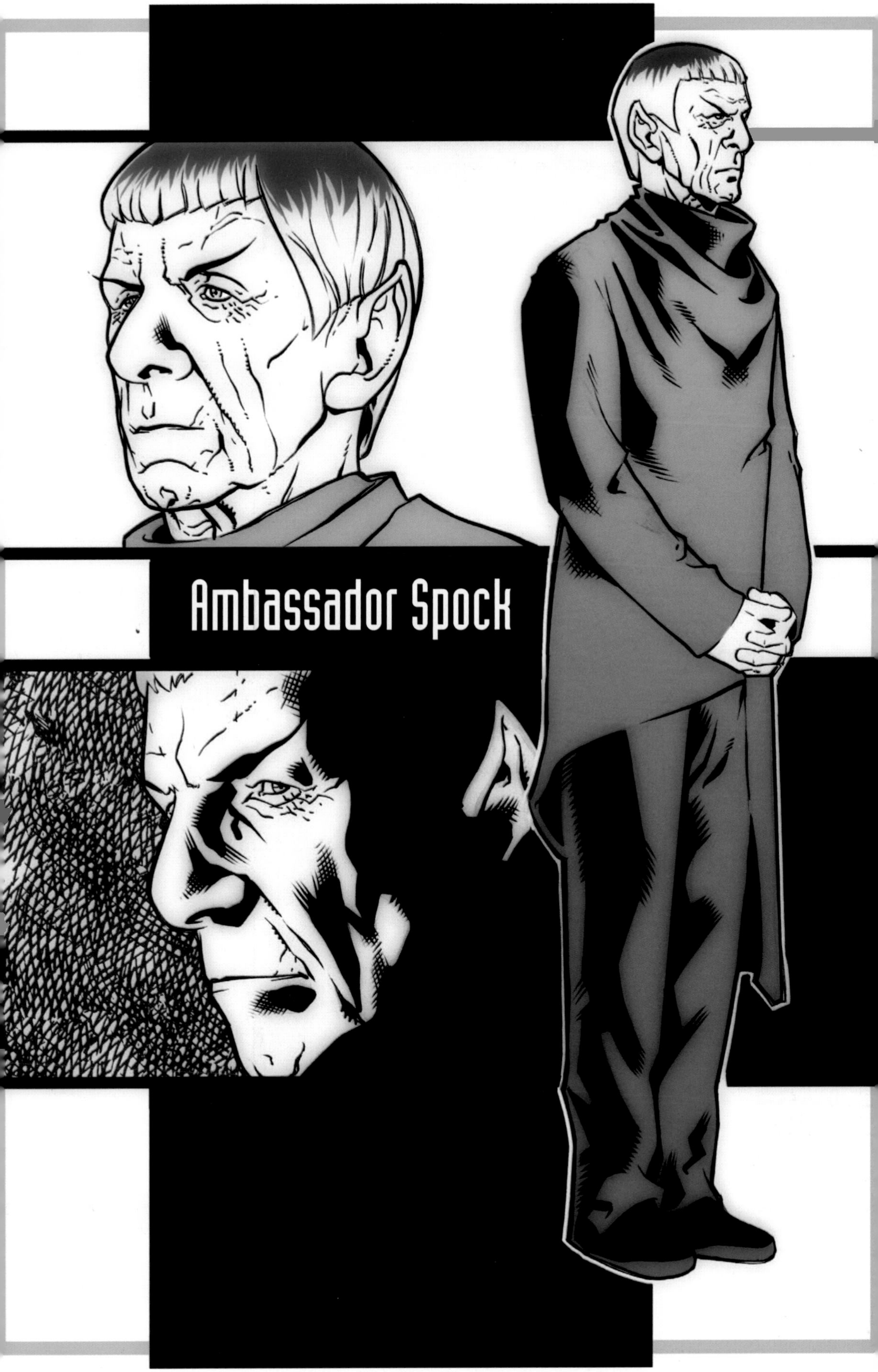
Ambassador Spock

Captain Data and Enterprise Crew

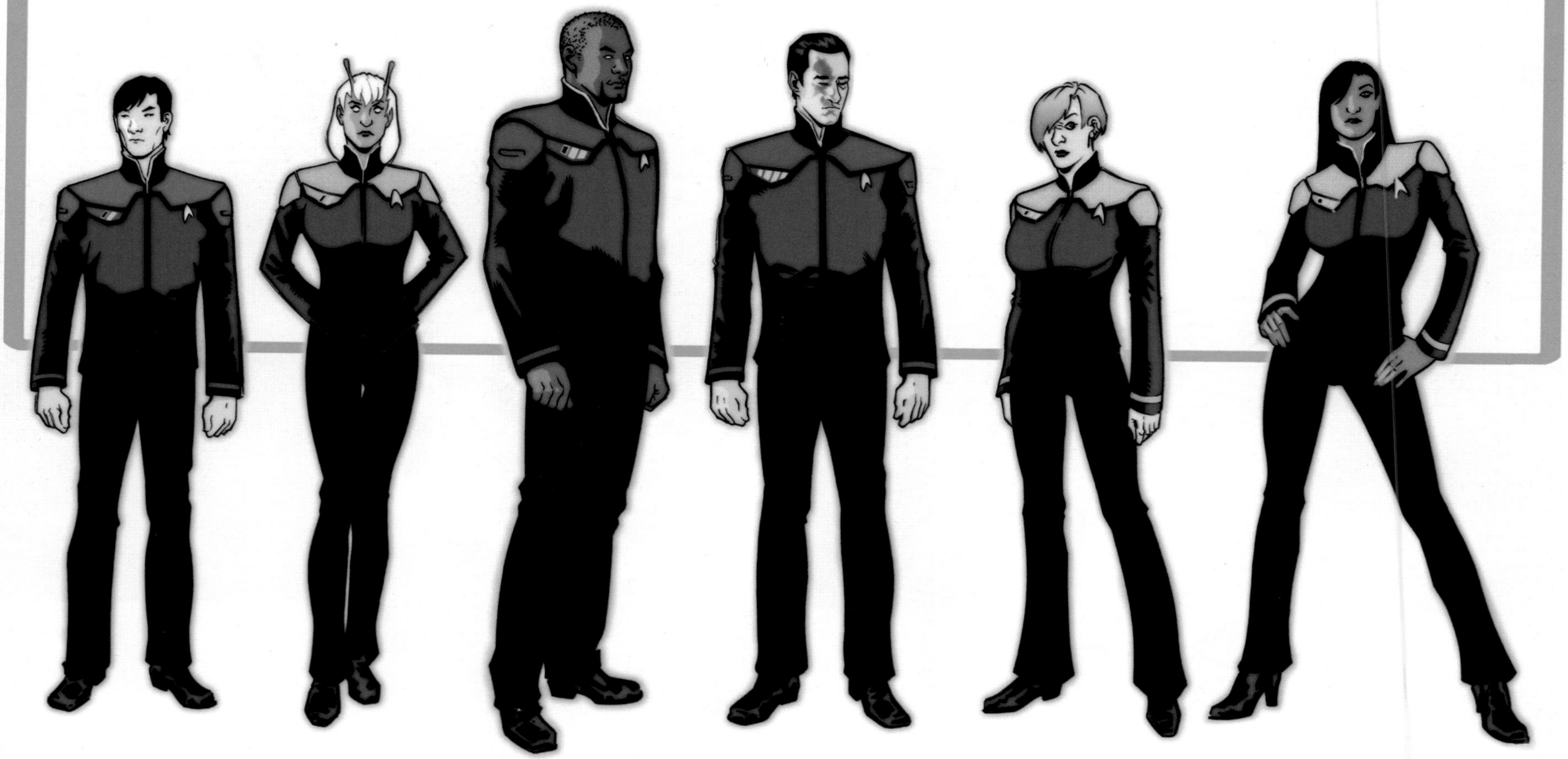